TIME, TWILIGHT, & ETERNITY

TIME, TWILIGHT, & ETERNITY

Finding the Sacred in the Everyday

Thom Rock

RESOURCE *Publications* · Eugene, Oregon

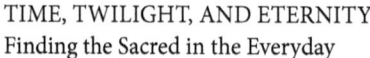

TIME, TWILIGHT, AND ETERNITY
Finding the Sacred in the Everyday

Copyright © 2017 Thom Rock. All rights reserved. Except for brief quotations in critical publications or reviews, no part of this book may be reproduced in any manner without prior written permission from the publisher. Write: Permissions, Wipf and Stock Publishers, 199 W. 8th Ave., Suite 3, Eugene, OR 97401.

Resource Publications
An Imprint of Wipf and Stock Publishers
199 W. 8th Ave., Suite 3
Eugene, OR 97401

www.wipfandstock.com

PAPERBACK ISBN: 978-1-5326-1780-5
HARDCOVER ISBN: 978-1-4982-4278-3
EBOOK ISBN: 978-1-4982-4277-6

Manufactured in the U.S.A.   05/03/17

All scripture quotations, unless otherwise indicated, are taken from the Holy Bible, New International Version®, NIV®. Copyright ©1973, 1978, 1984, 2011 by Biblica, Inc.™ Used by permission of Zondervan. All rights reserved worldwide. www.zondervan.com The "NIV" and "New International Version" are trademarks registered in the United States Patent and Trademark Office by Biblica, Inc.™

Scripture quotations marked (NRSV) are from the New Revised Standard Version Bible, copyright © 1989 the Division of Christian Education of the National Council of the Churches of Christ in the United States of America. Used by permission. All rights reserved.

The Qur'anic quotations contained herein are from the Saheeh International translation. Saheeh International, *The Qur'an: English Meanings and Notes,* Riyadh: Al-Muntada Al-Islami Trust, 2001–2011; Jeddah: Dar Abul-Qasim 1997–2001.

For Jim, always
and ever more

I am convinced there are hours of Nature, especially of the atmosphere, mornings and evenings, address'd to the soul.

—Walt Whitman

Day unto day utters speech, and night unto night shows knowledge.

—Psalm 19:2

'Tis Miracle before Me—then—'Tis Miracle behind—between.

—Emily Dickinson

Contents

A Twilight Litany | ix
Acknowledgements | xi
Sunrise, Sunset: An Overture | xiii

PART ONE
Before
    Light/Years | 5
    The Hours | 8
    In the Beginning | 20
    The Time of Our Lives | 26
    Ordinary Time | 37
    Already/Not Yet | 48

Vespers
    Time and Again | 57
    Night Flowers | 61
    Still Life | 67
    Burning the Midnight Oil | 79

ENTR'ACTE
Night
    Dark Matters | 89

PART TWO
Lauds
    First Light | 107
    The Eternal Now | 114
    House of Breath | 119
    The Fullness of Time | 128

AFTER
Afterglow | 137

Bibliography | 141

A Twilight Litany

Painter of the blue-blown sky; Glory the heavens declare
Turner of night and day; Sacred threshold, school of prayer
Wild eye of the universe; Steadfast witness, always there
Reminder of mystery; Eternal flame, celestial flare
Not quite night and neither day; In-between beyond compare
Palace in time; Sabbath sky, cathedral of air
Planet-sustaining atmosphere; Jewel of the heavens, commonplace yet rare
Spiraling chime of time; Unending hymn, neither here nor there,
Whose verse is twilight and chorus the dawn
As you kindle the clouds, let your radiance light the lamp of my heart
That I may see
Open my eyes to unbidden beauty and everyday grace
Build your house of breath in me; may each breath I take remind me of eternity
And that I am here
I am here
May gratitude be always on my lips and in my heart
Let my thanks rise as incense
Every day
As your ancient light breaks open the horizon, let my prayers rise and fall
Wave upon wave
Until they break on still other shores
In the mystery of everyday rising and setting, set me free
Of my assumptions and presumptions—of darkness and light
That I may begin
(Again)

Acknowledgements

While twilight gave me a time in which I might pay attention to prayer in my life, I am profoundly grateful for a welcoming place and tradition in which to ground that practice. For me that place is the community of Saint Mark's, Newport and the Episcopal Church in Vermont. The cadence and tempo of our prayer life together—from softly still and deeply reflective moments to exhilarating jazz evensong—played an important part in shaping not only this book but also continues to shape my heart.

One of the greatest charms of twilight is that it allows us to see certain bodies that appear to shine more brightly in that magic moment, although they are always present somewhere in the universe. In that light, I remember here with great fondness the late poet Jane Kenyan, though our orbits intersected only briefly. Decades after our first meeting, her kind encouragement to put pen to paper has remained with me—time travelling, as it were—and I have thought of her often as I wrote these pages or stood beneath the painted sky.

Amidst the firmament of people it takes to make a book, I would like to thank the constellation that is Wipf and Stock Publishers. I am especially grateful to Matthew Wimer, for his adept oversight of the project, and Brian Palmer for coordinating all the moving pieces with utmost professionalism and patience.

Lastly, I am profoundly thankful for my partner in life and in all things, without whom this book would never have seen the light of any day—and I would be truly in the dark. Jim, you are ever my Polaris: my true north and guiding star.

Sunrise, Sunset: An Overture

I cannot say exactly when sky-watching merged with my prayer life, only that at some point I began to find it difficult to separate my own rising to watch the sun rise quietly each dawn with my whispering a morning prayer, or my stopping to admire the spectacle of sunset and my pausing to give thanks in the dusky twilight. I'm certainly not the first to bend my knees in the gloaming, and hardly alone. For generations and cultures around the globe and across the ages, twilight has always been a sacred hour. Just as the sun gradually rises, so too have believers and seekers the world over.

Since the dawn of time there have always been sky-watchers. I should think there always will be. How could there not be? From the loveliness of an extraordinarily ordinary blue-sky day to the star-strewn night the heavens above have always fascinated us. And perhaps at no other time more so than those painted moments in between, when it isn't quite yet night, nor is it day. It was in those marginal hours of dawn and dusk, the twice-daily edges of day becoming night becoming day again, that I first began to pay careful attention to prayer in my life and my life in prayer—and to consciously make space for it every day. And as I did, I began to see that not only do so many people from so many different traditions pray, but we all pray by the same rising and setting sun—and the edges of our religions are not as sharp and distinct as some would have us believe.

The Book of Psalms in the Hebrew Bible speaks often of prayer at fixed times, especially at the twilight moments of morning and evening. Dawn and dusk have long been considered holy by many Hindus. The Holy Qur'an states in lovely language that the faithful should pray and give praise at eventide: "in the late afternoon and when the day begins to decline . . ." and again "when ye rise in the morning" (*The Qur'an*, Sura ar-Rūm 30:17–18). And Jesus often sought out twilight as a time and place for prayer (Mark 1:35; 6:46; Matt 14:23). In addition to the Christian command to "pray always" (1 Thess 5:16–18; Eph 6:18), many have knowingly, or unknowingly heeded the advice of Cyprian, the third-century martyred bishop of Carthage, who wrote of the necessity of prayer "at the sunsetting" and decline of day.

Indeed, there is nothing quite like the human body at prayer—naming, thanking, beseeching, proclaiming, wondering, remembering, praising, longing, belonging, returning. We bend our human bodies into one of the innumerable shapes of prayer: we fall to our knees, or sit cross-legged, or we stand and raise our hands to our hearts or to the sky; we light a candle or lamp, or we whisper into the dark; we lift our voices, or bow down and kiss the ground; we whirl around, or press our palms together, or fold our fingers into any number of age-old gestures.

The Talmud, the long-revered and authoritative compendium of Jewish law and custom, says, "Every blade of grass has an angel bending over it saying, 'grow, grow!'" (Midrash Rabba, Bereshit 10:6). Islam teaches: "For every soul there is a guardian watching it" (*The Qur'an*, aṭ-Ṭāriq 86:4). I have felt the same more than once standing in the twilight: that some divine source or conduit was leaning nearer than usual to whisper something in *my* ear. Each day's sunrise and sunset has become for me a pair of painted parentheses between which I try to hear and discern the holy sentences of my life unfolding in time. Sometimes I listen and pay attention. Many times I do not, and rush headlong and mindlessly into the next moment as the gorgeous colors of sunrise or sunset slide unnoticed into just another day or night in ordinary time.

Gradually though, the lesson began to dawn in me—slowly, incrementally, like the sun itself rises—as I began to consider that maybe what really matters isn't what happens before or after any sunrise or sunset so much as what we do in between each rising and setting: that our everyday moments in ordinary time are, in fact, the point of the matter. We ought to marvel at the commonplace, as Confucius observed so very long ago. And yet we seldom pause to even pay attention to our most ordinary moments, not to mention hallow them. Our minutes and hours and days all too often slip away completely unnoticed.

Meanwhile the sacred unfolds, if it unfolds anywhere, in ordinary time.

Where else would it?

This book is about that unfolding, and not only through the physics and optics of any twilight hour or rising or setting sun, but through our

Sunrise, Sunset: An Overture

own rising and setting—and rising again; about time and eternity and being present; about prayer and gratitude and the daily practice of resurrection; about beginnings and endings . . .

and beginning again.

In the transient, twin twilights of each day I unwittingly crafted my own version of what, in the Christian monastic tradition is called the Daily Office or the Liturgy of the Hours. Pre-eminent in that tradition are the prayer hours of Vespers and Lauds, said in the evening and at dawn respectively. Along the way, as I began to wonder about time and eternity I also began to wonder about the many boundaries we place around time. Exactly when does the glimmering vesper light of dusk become night's darkness, for example, or the welcome light of dawn drift into the plain old light of day? When does the day actually begin? (A seemingly simple question with more than one answer.) Or for that matter, what is a "day," one of the most basic measurements of time in our lives?

In many religious traditions the day begins not with the dawn but in the gloaming with the approaching night, with the evening dusk, at sunset—or in a word, twilight. The pages that follow are arranged to echo that same ancient pattern and rhythm. Part One is tinted with images of the evening twilight and explores our relationship with time. Vespers and other evening prayers, as well as the practice of keeping a Sabbath, are invoked. Part Two, is painted with the first light of dawn and the gratitude of Lauds, and looks at the physical and spiritual practices of wakefulness and attentiveness, and the rich tradition of discovering the eternal in the present. Between Vespers and Lauds the night sky always awaits with its stars and all that darkness in which they burn. Accordingly, in the Entr'acte—"Night"—I explore the role that darkness has played for so many seekers of illumination.

For me, observing the liminal hours of twilight has become less a discipline to keep and more an opportunity to listen closely for the sacred every day, and a reminder to fully inhabit my life in time as well as space. At their best, my prayerful twilights have been times of reason and reflection and revelation: the marvel and wonder of astronomy and physics and prayer and poetry all at once. Indeed, there have been some memorable skies along the way, spectacular sunsets that come readily to mind. Although it's tempting to want to extend those memorable twilit hours, to preserve forever their remarkable colors somehow, I know the sun will surely set and rise again.

Sunrise, Sunset: An Overture

And just as surely as there was, in the beginning, a day without any yesterday, there will come a time for each of us when there will be a day without a tomorrow.

In the end all we really have is our material and mortal bodies in time and space.

I have come to believe that twilight is so much more than optics alone. Dusk and dawn are moments when the curtains of Creation are briefly pulled back to reveal a glimpse of how everything rises and returns, including us; that we are not mere accidental combinations of stardust and happenstance elements, but implausibly and wonderfully *made*. The twin twilights of night becoming day and day becoming night reveal that we are never still or stuck but always beginning; that what holds this spinning universe together is not only gravity, but relationship and becoming.

That our salvation is in the everyday acts of rising and falling—

—and rising again.

And that there is much holiness in these ordinary, extraordinary acts.

PART ONE

Before

Light/Years

I.

Begin with cosmic calculation.

A star not much different than billions of others, a blue planet spinning in its orbit, a thin blanket of oxygen swaddling that star-struck ball... and us. Between the star and the planet, between the star and us: approximately ninety-three million miles. It takes more than eight minutes for the star's light, traveling at 186,000 miles per second, to navigate the darkness between and alight upon our faces.

The planet spins, tilted on its axis just so, and there is evening, and there is day. First the night, then the light—every dawn, the light—and after the light: night.

Begin with a moon circling the planet that is circling the sun; begin with reflection, with gravity and grace, with tides that rise and fall and rise up.

(Again)

Begin with revolution: Twenty-four hours, a measure of time, a day.

Multiply by 365.242199, the time it takes for the blue planet to make one complete circuit around the star and we get a year—time past, time present, time future—begin here: with the distance and duration of stars, the transit and timelessness of light. How everything depends on the tilt, the spin, the orbit—the circling around, irrevocably bound to each other.

And on spinning through space so fast we don't even know we are moving.

II.

Or begin with the end in which is our beginning, no "before" or "after" and yet we are born and we live and we die. Begin with the ancient light that reaches our eyes from our next nearest star which, being so many light-years away, will have left that sun more than four years ago—a star-beam reaching back in space more than twenty-five trillion miles.

Wherever we look we look backward in time: what was, what might have been. Time does not pass...

We do.

We know time only from the fleeting flight of things. Time doesn't simply fall like sand through an hourglass, we sieve it like powdered sugar dusted over flaked memories. Every breath and every moment is an end and a beginning; every person an epigraph and epitaph and that—*that* is where we start.

And where we depart...

Begin with us turned around just so, always looking over our shoulders, eternally saying goodbye. We are put here a little while that we may learn to bear the light of love, the Romantics declared. But we love what vanishes; it is time's ineluctable beams we cannot bear. The bygone days of days gone by, time gone by. Time irretrievable, irredeemable—time since, time without—time then and there...

And then again.

Begin with the brevity of—the urgency of—life. Begin with trajectory.

Begin with the fire of time in which we burn.

III.

Or begin with the sky on fire, begin with a word: sunset—another: gloaming. A bouquet of time arranged just so, a vase full of evening: sprays of starlight, night branches, a sprig of sunshine.

A single long-stemmed moment.

A perfect blue hour where we measure space with our hearts and love is that measure, where time is elastic and our passions expand it—time present, time immemorial.

Four o'Clocks ticking out their fragrance. Moonflowers and starflowers and morning glories clutching and clinging—their curling tendrils, their vining stems pulling them up to the light. A sunflower: its golden face chasing after the burning transit of a distant star in the sky. The blue gentian and forget-me-nots whispering pure words from the mountain-slopes of another time, another place.

Van Gogh arranging twilight in a sky blue vase:
Still / Life (the clutch, the cling)
Begin here, begin now. Begin always.

The Hours

We take the tick or digital sweep of the clock for granted, but long before it reigned over a global marketplace or became the tyrannical ruler of our time-torn lives it is today, the clock was a simple call to community and prayer. Before we ever gave time a face, sticks of incense and strings of beads fragrantly kept track of our holy moments as they measured the length of our prayers, and therefore our hours. They still do in ashrams, temples, and churches around the world. But this measure of time contained too much variability; tempo and cadence could easily skew any prayerful hour. More precise timekeeping could be found in the waning wax of a burning candle, or the steady drops of dripping water, or even grains of sands through the narrow opening of an "hourglass." While abstract time—invisible, intangible, immaterial—was far from concrete, we quickly learned that it cast an overarching shadow over all of our days nevertheless. The lengthening or shortening shadows cast by a perpendicular rod, spike, or pin set in the sun more reliably measured the day-lit hours.

Telling time by shadows was all well and good by the light of day, but what about when there was no source of illumination, when everything was shadow? When the shadows were breathing down our necks from all around?

FACING TIME

Perhaps our earliest ancestors hoped the dark hours didn't count, but the perennial problem was how to accurately keep track of prayer time through the night. Beyond the command to "pray always" (1 Thess 5:16–18; Eph 6:18), there were times when it was good to know what time it was, even if it was in the middle of the night. Whoever had the night watch, though, more often than not failed to keep his eyes open and the community inevitably and unknowingly slept through the hours—and their prayers—in the dark.

Primitive sundials eventually gave way to the more elaborate contraptions of cogs and wheels we would more readily recognize as a "clock" today. They may not have looked anything like our wristwatches, not to mention the digital read-outs of the screens and devices we seem to take for granted these days, but they were in fact the technical wonders of their day. Still, these earliest timepieces were not meant to remind one of time, but of eternity. Or, as Rabbi Abraham Joshua Heschel would much later note, the everlasting is to be found not beyond time but within it: "The days of our lives are representatives of eternity rather than fugitives," he wrote, "and we must live as if the fate of all time would totally depend on a single moment."[1] Likewise, the nineteenth-century Transcendentalists of New England found an active "correspondence" between the spiritual realm and the most ordinary daily experiences; that the hum of the holy could always be heard in the humdrum. For them the ordinary day was not merely an observable unit of time wrested from the clock or calendar, but a spiritual example to emulate: "You must become a day yourself," Emerson wrote.[2]

The first clocks had no hands at all, as their sole function was simply to remind monks to pray always, day and night. Only eventually did we lend time a hand—and only one—to mark the hours. The first minute hand didn't show up on clock faces until sometime in the sixteenth century, gaining greater popularity almost a century after that when the corrective and steady swing of the pendulum regulator was added to most clockworks. Obsessed as we are nowadays over speed and seconds, our ancestors seemed relatively unconcerned with those slimmest divisions of time. The thin line of the second hand didn't show up on clock faces until much later in the day.

The ubiquitous clock's religious beginnings are ironic: intended to assist the monastic in moving beyond time, the clock ultimately took the eternal and made of it something temporal; bound timelessness to time itself. Meant to mark time for worshiping God, the pendulum gradually swung the other way and the clock became a god itself to be worshiped. The word "clock" echoes out from the Medieval Latin *clocca* and the Old French *cloque* to even earlier words that all meant "bell." The endless chime of time has always called to those that listen. The only reason any hour strikes any

---

1. Heschel, *Man Is Not Alone*, 205.
2. Emerson, *The Complete Works*, VII: 180.

number on any clock at all is that the passing of time has for so long been associated with the reverberating sound of mallet against metal.

Because the lives of committed monastics included praying at fixed times day and night, they invented the ceaselessly ticking, tolling machines that we now take for granted, but upon which the monks depended to govern the consistent ringing of the *clocca*, or prayer bells. When the monastery bells rang they drew attention to the interior present moment as well as eternity, calling the faithful everywhere—both those within the walls of the community as well as anyone within earshot. The bells have been mostly muted since then; we're left to our own devices now. Heads down, we individually and carelessly note what time it is on the faces and screens of the digital gizmos and gadgets that virtually rule our lives today.

In each of the world's great religions, praise of the holy revolves around the disciplined and sanctified use of time. And all the faithful everywhere gather especially and intentionally at twilight—at dusk and at dawn—to sing praise to Whatever or Whomever created this clockwork and mind-bogglingly complex universe. The Book of Psalms in the Hebrew Bible speaks often of prayer at fixed times, especially at the twilight moments of morning and evening, and the famous story of Daniel in the Lion's Den revolves around the prophet's commitment to pray to his God morning, noon, and night (Dan 6:10). Sabbath begins and ends in twilight. Likewise, ritual fasting in Islam is measured from dawn to dusk. Muslims pray five times a day from early morning to evening to night. Both formal and informal prayer services have been constructed around morning and evening in almost every Christian denomination. The moments on either side of sunrise are considered especially auspicious for prayer, meditation, practicing forgiveness, and reciting excerpts from sacred scripture in the Hindu tradition, as are the evening hours. Considered sacred times, dawn and dusk are when many Hindus perform one of the oldest extant liturgies in the world: *Sandhyāvandana*—literally, "salutation to the transition moments of the day" (meaning the twin twilights of dawn and dusk).

Twilight, it turned out, was a naturally occurring twice-daily gong; the dependable bell-strike of dawn and dusk the perfect call to prayer.

Whether at cockcrow or the call of the cricket, sunrises and sunsets strike an ancient chord in us that wakes something primal and attentive within and so it is, perhaps, that these two astronomical events have found their place as key reminders of attention, prayer, and mindfulness in every world religion. Setting aside and honoring fixed times for prayer is never convenient or easy, though; prayer is neither routinely our first instinct upon rising in the morning, nor necessarily the last thing we think of at the end of a busy day. But what all spiritual traditions recognize is that to engage in that practice is to make every moment holy, sanctifying time itself—and therefore our lives.

"Seven times a day I praise you. . ." the Psalmist sang (Ps 119:164). Much later Christian monks based their call to prayer throughout the day in part on that verse from the Hebrew Bible, praying at least that often. The number seven is a meaningful one in scripture, though, often associated with perfection or the infinite. The seven-fold prayer passage could also be interpreted to mean that we should simply pray always, all the time. After the ascension of Jesus, who also prayed in the morning and in the evening (Mark 1:35; 6:46; Matt 14:23), there were many who "constantly devoted themselves to prayer" (Acts 1:14) as they kept one eye trained on the heavens above, awaiting his imminent return.

In the beginning was always twilight, darkness, and the hope of a new day. We begin as sky-watchers who come from a long line of sky-watchers before us.

STARRY, STARRY NIGHT

Nightfall, and therefore the timing of either beginning or ending one's evening prayer, has long been associated with the moment when at least three small stars can be discerned in the darkening sky. The ever-twinkling stars made for a good marker of slippery time and uncertain prayer: ever-present—and always just beyond our grasp. But marking the exact moment when the long-awaited stars appeared, or for that matter the precise time of sunset or sunrise, the gradual shift from day to night to day, was highly subjective. It still is: there can be about as many variables as—well, as there are stars in the sky. In fact our deep longing and desire for the holy is linked quite literally to the stars. The etymology of the word "desire" leads back to the Latin *de sidere*, or "from the stars," which in turn can also be thought of as meaning "awaiting what the stars will bring."

The Talmud, the seemingly inexhaustible treasury of a wealth of Hebraic law and custom, says that three *medium*-sized stars visible in the sky signify when nightfall (or "starshine" as it more poetically puts it) begins. But even according to Jewish law, this astronomical event can arrive anywhere from twenty minutes to more than an hour after sunset—not to mention the factor of from what point on the spinning globe one happens to be looking up at the stars. The Talmud's evening skies over ancient Babylonia and Israel were quite different from those visible from modern-day Taipei or Toronto—or even above a fiddler balanced precariously at sunrise or sunset on the roof of a milkman's humble home in the fictional *shtetl* of Anatevka on the eve of an eternal Sabbath in a very real Imperial Russia.[3]

Some rabbis opted for a more flexible determination of the arrival of night as when the sky was dark except for the faintest glow of the gloaming on the western horizon, a reckoning not unlike that most Muslims follow. In Islam, the ṣalāt al-maġrib, or evening prayer, is the fourth of five formal daily prayers and can be prayed anytime from just after the sun sets until all but the slightest twilight color has disappeared from the sky and darkness is complete—at which point the time for night prayers begins.

It wasn't only rabbis and imams and theologians that were counting on the stars, though. Poets and painters, scientists and mathematicians have long read the night sky for illumination. The poets were, perhaps, the first to call dusk the "blue hour"—a moment in-between sunset and night and the earliest pinpricks of astral light. Dickens sanctified the phenomenon and called it *blessed* twilight. The French perfumer Jacques Guerlain tried to capture the fragrance of that elusive time in "l'Heure Bleue," the scent he created to pay tribute to the moment when, in his lovely words, "the sky has lost the sun, but has not yet gained the stars."[4] In fact the canon of the firmament has produced more than a few star-struck believers—poets like Blake, Poe, Emerson, and Thoreau; scientists like Einstein, Kepler, Hutton, and Hubble. The Dutch artist Vincent van Gogh, when he had need for church, simply went outside and worshipped beneath the vast dome of night. Before he ever completed what would surely come to be one of his most celebrated paintings—*The Starry Night*—he wrote in one of his many surviving letters about his desire to express human hope by indelibly painting the stars; to portray the eagerness of the human soul by capturing the colors of sunset.[5]

---

3. I refer, of course, to Tevye the Dairyman, the central character in an eponymous story originally written by Sholem Aleichem, and the opening scene of its more widely known theatrical and film incarnations, "Fiddler on the Roof." See Aleichem, *Tevye the Dairyman*; and Norman Jewison et al., *Fiddler on the Roof*.

4. In Hoeppe, *Why the Sky Is Blue*, 236.

5. An idea he expressed in a letter to his brother Theo. See "Letter 531" in van Gogh, *The Complete Letters*, III:26. Perhaps more famously, Vincent expressed in later correspondence his struggle between organized religion and personal worship: "That does not

The Hours

BEGIN AGAIN

"Always we begin again." These four gracious words travel down through the ages to us from when they were first penned by Saint Benedict of Nursia sometime around the middle of the sixth century. They are a part of a set of precepts by which medieval monks lived in communion with each other and by which many contemporary monastics still live. A code of conduct known today as the Rule of St. Benedict, it governed every manner in which a monk lived, from sleep to work, eating, speaking, and prayer.[6] This document has been and continues to be a unique and influential treatise on the disciplined and sanctified use of time. At its core: a regular schedule of "hours" at which the religious attended to specific activities as mundane as eating or working, and as profound as communal worship and prayer. Either way, the life was routine—and austere. Nowhere in the Christian tradition was the rhythm of daily prayer more refined and more closely associated with measured time than in the monastic communities founded by Saint Benedict.

Before Benedict there was certainly a kind of calendar as it then existed in the Christian faith: a loose collection of feast days associated with saints and martyrs, and holy days linked to the events of the life, death, and resurrection of Jesus Christ. But Benedict gave equal attention to *every* day of the year, assigning a specific function and kind of work to each one—and then went on to sanctify every hour of every day. His philosophy is succinctly summed up in the community's over-arching motto of *ora et labora*—"pray and work." More than a mere fixation with measuring time, Benedict's Rule was meant to instill order and community, but also to test a seeker's spiritual stamina, faith, and willpower.

The monastery bells rang day and night, at which point the monks pulled themselves up from either the ground where they were diligently working, or the straw mats or wooden pallets on which they slept, and prayed. From Vigils in the middle of the night to morning prayer known as Matins or Lauds at sunrise; from Prime just after dawn to Terce mid-morning and Sext at midday; from None, or afternoon prayer, to Vespers just before sunset, every segment of every twenty-four-hour cycle was punctuated with prayer. Benedict even added an eighth service in the traditional cycle:

---

keep me from having a terrible need of—shall I say the word—religion. Then I go out at night to paint the stars." See "Letter 543" in ibid., III: 56.

6. See, for example, Kardong, *Benedict's Rule*, especially chapter 73; and McQuiston, *Always We Begin Again*.

Compline, a night prayer to be sung after dark. If the monks weren't working or praying, it seems they were studying scripture. The Psalms provided a constant measure to the monastics' every day. Their goal in marking time so regularly: to keep the attention of their ephemeral lives trained on the hereafter, living every hour *sub specie aeternitatis*—or from the perspective of eternity.

This pattern of prayer and scripture reading interwoven with the rest of life's ordinary moments has been variously called the daily or divine office, common prayer, fixed-hour prayer, the canonical hours, or the Liturgy of the Hours. But because time was then calculated by simply dividing the number of daylight hours by twelve—a remnant and imposition of the ruling Roman army—the actual length of the monks' divine hours of prayer differed depending on what time of the year it was. By whatever name, the hours stretched out lazily in the long summer sun; they were mercifully short in the cold, dark winter. The length of any "hour" was open to much interpretation and translation depending on one's location and season of the year—hardly the regular and rigid sixty minutes of our contemporary definition of what we think makes an hour. For our prayerful ancestors an "hour" was simply one-twelfth of whatever amount of daylight there was on any specific "day." The only times all the hours ever equaled the same length and approached exactly sixty minutes were the two days each year when heaven and earth perfectly aligned—the Spring and Autumn equinoxes—when there were exactly twelve equal hours of daylight and twelve of dark.

Regardless of what time of the year it was, the liturgical hours were always measured from sunrise or sunset. It seems our souls have always been drawn to the solar, never meant to be analogue or digital. The primal sunrise gave the office of Prime its name. Terce, or roughly "third," arrived three not-necessarily-sixty-minute-long "hours" after that astronomical event. Sext was said six hours after sunrise, and the mid-afternoon prayer of None was recited nine hours after sunrise. Vespers is always said before sunset; compline after. Similarly, many Jewish rituals that are to be performed at specific times are calculated with an eye to the sky and a special unit of time known as *sha'ah zmanit*, a proportional hour that takes into account one's location and the seasonal length of any day. Ultimately, saying there are only a certain amount of minutes in every hour is as deceptive as saying there is a calculable number of how many moments make a life.

The Hours

UNCOMMON: PRAYER

Something happens to time when it is routinely pierced by prayer. The earliest Christian monks knew this. The ancient Hebrews knew this. The ascetics and mystics of the Eastern traditions knew this. Which, for many of us, begs the question: why is it so darn difficult to incorporate routine prayer into our lives? Ironically, the answer we offer most often is time itself—or, more precisely, the lack thereof. We're just too busy, there's too much going on, and we have too many demands on our precious little time already. But if we're honest with ourselves, it's not only that we're just too busy to pray; we're also too occupied with what else might be going on. (We wouldn't want to miss out on anything, after all.) And let's face it, prayer isn't always thrilling. We too often think, hope, or expect that we will hear trumpets and cymbals sound when we pray, or even hear God speaking personally to us. But more often than not prayer is remarkably uneventful. We may have as an iconic image a romantic notion of medieval monks with quills in hand tirelessly scribing sacred scrolls with exotic colored inks and elegantly gilded illuminations. But the three Rs of the monastery were never reading, writing, nor 'rithmetic; they were regular, routine, and repeat.

Like the daily motions of the earth, the everyday rising and setting of the sun.

For the twelfth-century mystic Hildegard of Bingen, prayer meant breathing in and out the one constant breath of the universe. The twentieth-century French philosopher Simone Weil considered our absolute attention the same thing as prayer. Meister Eckhart said that if the only prayer we ever whispered was "thank-you," that would be enough. Kierkegaard likened laughter to a form of prayer. Ignatius of Loyola taught that anything turned in the direction of God is prayer. Indeed, an entire library would be required to contain our various definitions of prayer over time.

The simplest prayer I know is "Yes." Another one: "Trust."

Or the two Greek words at the very root of all Christian prayer: *Kyrie, eleison.*

"Lord, have mercy."

In the beginning has always been prayer. Because, as Mother Teresa clarified, "everything begins with prayer."[7]

---

[7] Mother Teresa expressed this sentiment many times and in many ways. See, for example, *The Joy in Loving*, 43; and throughout Stern, *Everything Starts from Prayer*.

Time, Twilight, and Eternity

As basic and imperative as that sounds, common prayer is still all too uncommon. If anything it seems to be becoming ever rarer. For some it is, perhaps, the word itself that gets in the way: The word "prayer" can evoke both positive as well as negative associations depending on one's experience of, and relationship to it. The same can be said of its alternatives, like mindfulness or meditation. Still, "prayer" seems most accurate at its roots; it comes from the Latin *precari*, meaning to ask earnestly. And in fact we more often than not tend to ask *for* something—a specific outcome ranging anywhere from good health and comfortable wealth to world peace—in our prayers. We naturally pray for the best outcome and relief from the alternative. And inevitably we never get all we really want. The result: prayer—not to mention God—can seem inconsistent and arbitrary at best.

But what if the truest form of intercession isn't praying *to* or *for*, but *with*? This can of course take the form of recitation, but there is also the Jewish notion of *mitzvah*, of "a good work." We can "do" as well as "say" our prayers. Muslims practice *ṣalāt*, an Arabic word that is often interchanged with its closest English equivalent: "prayer." But *ṣalāt* implies not only the stillness commonly associated with prayer but also supplication, a devotional integration of spiritual surrender with physical motion. "Pray without ceasing," Saint Francis of Assisi is supposed to have said, "if necessary, use words."

Ultimately, whatever form it takes, prayer does not necessarily alter the circumstances as much as it changes the perspective of the one who prays. We each and all would do well if our only prayer was the ceaseless question curious young children ask: "Why?"—and then lived out our precarious lives as provocatively as that ultimately unanswerable question. "We will not perish from lack of information," Rabbi Heschel wrote, "but only for want of appreciation: What we lack is not a will to believe but a will to wonder."[8]

Wondering why and knowing how are two very different postures, though. As children we naturally expressed our insatiable curiosity about the world and our place in it by constantly asking the seemingly simple, yet wonder-filled question: "Why?" Eventually—sadly—too many of us lose that holy curiosity and stop wondering altogether. Why *are* there stars in the sky? Why don't we see them during the day? Why is the night dark? If the stars are always shining then why isn't the night light? Always appearing to be about things we should all know, the innocent why's children ask

---

8. Heschel, *Man Is Not Alone*, 26.

are more often than not profound and probing questions that reveal ever more complex subtleties and seldom have definitive answers. The more we consider the question, the more we realize we don't have a clue what the answer is. So we fall back on the old standard: "Because."

This inevitably leads to the child's second most favorite question: "Because why?"

"Because that's the way things are," we say with as much authority as we can muster. "The night is dark because that's what night is."

And, of course this might work once or twice, until the curious expanding little mind catches on. So, we transpose the *why* into the more answerable *how* and explain the science or physics of something. But that still hasn't answered the question. We can always figure out how. It's the why that always leaves us wondering. I can study and come to understand, for example, the fascinating science and optics of how twilight interacts with the rods and cones of our eyes. But that doesn't come anywhere near answering what I think is the more interesting question of why the dawn or dusk stirs the soul or imagination so. That's something else entirely.

All our human nature ever really wants is a final answer. But the fact is any search for understanding is most productive when every question leads not to a succinct answer but to yet another even more interesting question. The most profound truths always feel more like beginnings than endings. All of this isn't to say that *how* cannot be a helpful question—it can be. Especially when asked in the context of such inquiries as "how do we know what we know?" or "how do we know something is real?" Or, "how can we be certain of a certain thing—of anything?" But then the answers to these questions probably have more to do with squirrely belief than actual proof. Further, they are about the difference between believing *that* something is or happened, versus believing *in* something as truth. Or as the poet Rilke famously suggested, about not seeking or finding the answers, so much as living out the questions themselves.[9]

Perhaps best known for his contributions to physics and mathematics, Sir Isaac Newton produced far more written materials on biblical interpretation. While he acknowledged the clutch of gravity and its role in the universe—the motions of the planets—he ultimately found (and admitted)

---

9. His oft-quoted advice to an aspiring poet: "Don't search for answers, which could not be given to you now, because you would not be able to live them. And the point is, to live everything. Live the questions now. Perhaps then, someday in the future, you will gradually, without even noticing it, live your way into the answer." In Rilke, *Letters to a Young Poet*, 46.

Time, Twilight, and Eternity

it could not explain who or what first set the planets in motion. Henry David Thoreau tried to keep two journals, one for recording "just the facts," and the other for more poetical musings. But he ultimately found the world full of poetry.[10] Science and religion operate in the same arena. They simply speak different languages: one a dialect of fact, the other a poetry of faith; one of knowing, the other of believing.

Truth is never singular.

There are forces in the universe which we do not, and cannot understand, despite our endless inquiry—forces that are not diminishing but expanding. Forces that bind atom to atom across time and space; forces like gravity that bring us into each other's orbit; forces that catch us when we fall and lift us up; forces that propel light through darkness faster than we can ever imagine. Some refer to the dynamic forces that are thought to move throughout the universe as Shakti. Others call those same forces Brahma, or Holy Spirit, or even God (by whatever name). Still others call this life-force Source, or the Absolute, or the Tao. For some the forces that both expand and hold together the universe are simply energy, light, and matter.

I use the word "prayer" to express the discipline of striving to pay attention to the why and speechless wonder of these forces. But there are plenty of other choices. If you're not comfortable with prayer, there's contemplation, concentration, careful observation, or even the call of the heart. For some putting one foot in front of the other can be prayer. Listening deeply is perhaps one of the most profound spiritual disciplines. I would no sooner presume to tell you what words to use when engaging with the eternal than how to do it. If a word gets in your way, translate it into something that has meaning for you and what you take seriously about life. The Sufi mystic Jalal al-Din Rumi famously noted there are hundreds of ways to kneel and kiss the ground. The Talmud states that it is permissible to pray in any language that you can understand. "Pray as you can," one Christian monastic adage councils, "not as you can't."

There is, in fact, a charming story from the Jewish tradition that speaks to this aspect prayer. There was once a young boy who wanted to

---

10. On February 18, 1852 he wrote in his journal: "I have a commonplace book for facts, and another for poetry, but I find it difficult always to preserve the vague distinction which I had in mind, for the most interesting and beautiful facts are so much more poetry and that is their success. They are transmuted from earth to heaven. I see that is my facts were sufficiently vital and significant—perhaps transmuted into the substance of the human mind—I should need but one book of poetry to contain them all." In Thoreau, *The Journal*, 114.

pray but did not yet know many Hebrew words; all he knew was the letters of the *aleph-beth*, or "alphabet," so that became his prayer. One day as he was praying what he knew—his letters—a rabbi heard him and asked why he prayed in that way. The wise little one declared, "The Holy One knows my heart. I give him the letters, and he puts the words together."

Eventually, the Benedictine sense of time overflowed the walls of medieval monasteries and the Liturgy of the Hours became a rhythm of life even for some who lived and worked in the distinctly secular villages beyond the religious compounds. Elegantly penned and bound Christian devotional manuscripts known as "Books of Hours" contained an abbreviated form of the Divine Office designed for the average lay person and were widely available and popular by the fifteenth century. The original daily planners, every appointment was with God. Their pages were comprised of a collection of litanies, prayers, psalms, and excerpts from the Gospels, and were considered palm-sized and portable cathedrals. The wide margins surrounding the elegant medieval calligraphy of each page's sacred text were often elaborately decorated with illustrations—illuminations—of the daily, the mundane, and the ordinary moments of everyday life.

If the mystics were right, as surely they were, and every creature is a book about God, then each moment is a letter in a sacred alphabet even if we don't yet understand the whole word. And every one of our hours is a holy chapter in the story of eternity—the story of us.

A book of ours.

In the Beginning

Whether the universe began as an enormous explosion of energy or was divinely spoken into existence, nothing we know or experience today was ever extant prior to that absolute flashpoint. Everything that matters—space, us, time—was set in motion as a result of that singular event. The genesis of the cosmos can be summed up in one word:

After.

God only knows what came before.

In the beginning was the word, and the word without a shadow of a doubt was *Light*. Ever since that primordial before-and-after either physics or grace has been unfolding: the everyday gift of a rising and setting sun. Except each sunset or sunrise is never really a solar event as much as it is a terrestrial one. The universe does not revolve around us, the sun does not rise. We turn toward or away from its light. Sunset would be more appropriately described as earth-spin on our skewed little planet. (Neither do we call it nightrise, even though that's also more accurate.) Night, after all, is nothing more than the shadow side of a rotating satellite in orbit around an illuminated source.

Still, watch the last bit of daylight slip over the horizon at any day's end, and it isn't difficult to imagine and feel why so many of our ancestors made gods and monsters out of the sun and the night.

Our very words belie what we fear: we exclaim, "*Tempus fugit,*" (Time flies) and "*Carpe diem,*" (Seize the day) whenever we mean to encourage each other to make our day-lit hours count. But when was the last time someone emboldened you to "*carpe noctem*," (seize the night)? We look for eternally blue skies in life, not some dark night of the soul. While we declare that daylight rises, night and darkness always seem to fall—they descend. We convince ourselves that the worst things always happen in the dead of night and tell ourselves everything will look better in the light of the day. And when that light arrives we sing ebulliently that morning has broken, as if it were the first day of creation. When night returns we lay our heads to sleep and pray to God our souls to keep.

"It is frightening to think how many things / are made and unmade with words," the poet Rilke wrote, "they are so far removed from us, / trapped in their eternal imprecision, / indifferent with regard to our most urgent needs."[1] We can say our genesis was etymological, or we can say it was biological—neither explanation ultimately satisfies. All words have a life of their own, abandoning us when we most need them and evading our grasp when we most desperately need something to hold on to. They are made not for us but for each other: a sentence is never complete, Saint Augustine keenly observed, "unless one word pass away when it has sounded its part, in order that another may succeed it."[2] And so we cannot imagine a beginning without an end, a before without an after, nor a light without a dark to put it in.

We could know an entirely other world, though (to paraphrase Wittgenstein, the great twentieth-century philosopher of language), if we simply spoke different words to each other. "Death and life are in the power of the tongue," the Hebrew Bible tells us (Prov 18:21). The sun did not rise only once at some primal beginning. Our story begins with *always*—with every day—not "once upon a time."

THEN AGAIN

Once upon a time there was no time. Whatever the word was in the beginning, in the beginning there was nothing: no light, no matter, no energy, no space or time... no anything.

Begin with something out of nothing—or before nothing. Begin before anything mattered. Begin with endless burning night, with the entire universe squeezed into the space of the nucleus of a single atom, with an inferno of becoming about to become. Begin with a mass of roiling hydrogen and helium—with primeval nuclei colliding and fusing and transforming—a furnace of confusion.

Begin with us, beginning.

Today, most astronomers agree on a figure of about thirteen-billion years (give or take a billion years or two) as the approximate age of the

---

1. Rilke, *The Poet's Guide to Life*, 130.
2. Augustine of Hippo, *The Confessions*, 52.

physical universe, a number that, in relation to our lived experience of time, is virtually incomprehensible. We might as well say the universe is as old as eternity. In fact, some physicists now refute the "Big Bang" theory and posit instead a so-called "Steady State" theory, or that the universe may indeed have no beginning at all. Which is kind of what the Bible says (and so many of the world's sacred scriptures say) about our beginnings in their more poetic original languages: not that something was or wasn't "in the beginning," but that we are part of a wonderfully mysterious beginning-less beginning that unfolds in a now that is somehow beyond now.

According to the *Tao Te Ching*, the classic Chinese text fundamental to the philosophy of Taoism, in the beginning was only Void, within which was That or the One which has no shape or sound yet is the origin of all origins—that which has no beginning and no end—and which Lao Tzu called the Tao, or Greatness, or the Great Integrity. Krishna referred to this same beginning-less beginning as an unknown and unknowable All. Similarly, the Gnostic Gospels talk about a time "before That-Which-Is ever became visible."[3] In one of the sacred Hindu texts known collectively as the Vedas, the great creation hymn in the Rig-Veda says of the earliest beginning:

> The non-existent was not, the existent was not: there was no realm of air, no sky beyond it. . . . Death was not then, nor was there aught immortal: no sign was there, the day's and night's divider. That One Thing, breathless, breathed by its own nature: apart from it was nothing whatsoever. Darkness there was: at first concealed in darkness this All was indiscriminate chaos. All that existed then was void and formless. . . (Rig-Veda 10.129.1–4).[4]

The Jewish mystical tradition of Kabbalah embraces the notion that a primordial Nothingness brought forth the beginning and the end at once. Rabbi Zalman Schachter-Shalomi said that a more rightful translation of the Hebrew words of Genesis 1:1, the very beginning of the Bible, would be "In *a* beginning," rather than "In *the* beginning"—that we are always beginning, a part of an ongoing story. Not once upon a time but all the time. Ultimately, that the beginning even ever was is a matter of faith, as the poet-priest John Donne pointed out: "*When* it was," he continued, "is a matter of reason, and therefore various and perplex'd."[5]

---

3. For Taoist, Hindu, and Gnostic references see, for example, Lao Tzu, *Tao Te Ching*, 51, 201–202; and Hooper, *Jesus, Buddha, Krishna, Lao Tzu*, 53, 55.

4. Griffith, *Hymns of the Rig-Veda*, II, 621–22.

5. In Eiseley, *The Firmament of Time*, 1.

In the Beginning

The Jewish writer Martin Buber begins his classic treatise on the philosophy of dialogue, *I and Thou*, with: "In the beginning was relation,"[6] a thoughtful re-arrangement of what is perhaps the most familiar "in the beginning," the one that introduces the New Testament's Johanine gospel, itself a re-arrangement of the Hebrew Bible's Book of Genesis. The word that allows for such re-consideration is the word *word* itself—or more rightly, *logos*, the Greek original long since translated into the English word with which so many of us have become so familiar. *Logos,* like so many words, doesn't really have a precise equivalent in language other than its mother tongue. "Word" is a perfectly appropriate translation, but so is meaning or message. Teaching, communication, and wisdom can all work, too. One can even make the case that in the beginning was the reason, or the story, or the law . . . or even the thing. That's the thing about words: hold them up to the light and they reveal how multi-faceted they are, like so many diamonds—every face reflecting the light at a different angle—the clearest, most brilliant ones hard and costly and rare.

Time is perhaps the most faceted diamond, the shiniest gemstone in our dictionary. It is not linear but prismatic. Indivisible and atomic, time can bend light, space, and definition. Hours can stand still even as the clock goes on ticking. Time can fly, like a hummingbird: an emerald and ruby jewel on whirring wings—a glimpse . . .

. . . and gone.

FLOWING TIME

We tend to view time, with all of its perceived beginnings and endings—its *before's* and *after's*—as progressing in a certain order and in a certain direction, all too often skipping right over now in favor of what was or what might be. We begin at a beginning and end at a conclusion. We make of time a river upon whose banks we sit and watch it flowing past:

Time irreversible.

In fact, before we ever thought of time in mathematical, astronomical, or even quantum mechanical terms we thought about it in agricultural ones. We paid particular attention to whatever river was nearby. For the Ancient Egyptians, life itself—both this side of death and after it—depended on the River Nile. The river was their calendar stretching over more than four thousand miles and marked three key seasons of life: flooding,

---

6. Buber, *I and Thou*, 18.

growth, and harvest. Water and rivers flow throughout the Hebrew Bible, and at least one reference, the name of a Canaanite month, reveals further connection between flowing water and flowing time: *Ethanim*, the month of steady flowing, when only the most perennial streams still held water (1Kgs 8:2).

The first book of the Hebrew Bible tells of a primordial river that flowed out of Eden to the four corners of the earth (Gen 2). The New Testament concludes with a vision of another river, one that flows by the throne of God and by which Eden will be restored (Rev 22:1), a river that circles back to the original headwaters described in the Book of Genesis. The Ganges River is sacred to Hindus, the most auspicious place to perform one's devotional meditation and bathing, not to mention the whispered offering of a sunset *puja*, or prayer. In fact, that religion has seven holy rivers and many others whose waters are significant. A dip in any one of those waters is thought to cleanse one of sin, an act that reverberates with the splash and dunk of Christian baptism, first performed also in a river, as we know from the story of John and Jesus on the shores of the Jordan in the desert country of Judea.

According to the revelation of the desert Prophet of Islam, Muhammad (peace be upon him), in the beginning was not light but water—the life-sustaining connection of a single atom of oxygen to two of hydrogen combined just so.

In fact, time is a river whose current is swift and flows in one direction only through all three Abrahamic faiths: Christianity, Islam, and Judaism. Along its banks our salvation unfolds in an orderly progression—eschatologically—from the creation of the world to our fall and redemption; from judgment to last days to heavenly paradise. In other religions time, and therefore life—not to mention divine grace—isn't quite as linear. Besides, no river's course is perfectly straight. Just as our own stream of consciousness can take surprising twists and turns, any river always finds its way by whatever route necessary back to its source: the sea. Eventually, as Norman Maclean wrote in his short story, "all things merge into one, and a river runs through it."[7]

Buddhism and Hinduism, amongst other traditions, view time's passing in more cyclical terms. Rivers flow out in every direction from the primal headwaters of the Navajo creation story. Taoism teaches to live in harmony with a concept of time that is more like a repeating rhythm than a river. If time is a river it is one that flows in more than one direction.

---

7. Maclean, *A River Runs Through It*, 104.

In the Beginning

Or at least, as James Joyce would have us believe in his cyclical and final masterpiece *Finnegan's Wake*,[8] one that has no "once upon a time" or "the end" but recirculates all along life's ...

... riverrun, an image rooted in the ancient philosophies of Heraclitus, Plato, and Marcus Aurelius who each noted in their own way that we cannot step twice into the same river. The thirteenth-century Buddhist poet/priest Chōmei echoed their insights in the opening line of his classic tale of impermanence: "the flowing river never stops and yet the water never stays the same."[9] When we come to the banks of any river we find ourselves at the very shores of space and time.

Try as we might we cannot dam time; neither the clock nor the calendar slows its flood. "Like as the waves make toward the pebbled shore / so do our minutes hasten to their end."[10] Nothing stands still. Modern physics reveals that the very building blocks of matter are not passive and inert, but constantly dancing with everything else in the universe. Every atom vibrates, pulses with energy, oscillates with the absorption and emission of existence itself. Everything is in the dynamic process of both being *and* becoming. Change is the eternal constant; life is liquid, riverine. Time can slow to a trickle—or overflow its banks and become a torrent. Regardless of the direction the river flows it branches into tributaries we call the past, the present, and the future—the rivulets Augustine called memory, attention, and expectation—what was, is, and will be.

The Romans saw the Milky Way—the great river of stars above our heads—as the luminous wake of a celestial ship. To the Māori of New Zealand it is a canoe crossing the sea. In Chinese astronomy, it is a celestial river; people of Eastern Asia believed it was the Silvery Stream of Heaven. The Aboriginal People of Australia see the band of stars as a river in the "skyworld," and in Hindu myth it is *Akasaganga*, which means "the (Ganges) River of the Sky."

Something in us has always understood the implications of the stars streaming by above our heads; the flickering, fleeting firelight of life's timelessness.

In the beginning was flow, flux ... change.

And ever since: nothing has been the same.

---

8. In what is the beginning and end—and beginning again—of his literary classic: "A way a lone a last a loved a long the / riverrun." Joyce, *Finnegan's Wake*, 628, 3.

9. Chōmei, *Hōjōki*, 19.

10. Shakespeare, "Sonnet 60.1–2" in *The Complete Works*, 1606.

The Time of Our Lives

We say the existence of eternity cannot be proven, that it makes no logical sense. But the same can be said of the measurement of something we've agreed to call, for lack of a better word, time. There was a time when we simply looked to the sky to guide us—when the planet spun, tilted on its axis just so, and there was evening and there was day—and that was enough. Or, on a more practical, corporeal level, we looked to our stomachs to tell us, for example, when it was time to eat. We didn't have a name for it back then, but the suprachiasmatic nucleus and preoptic areas in the part of our brains known as the hypothalamus told us when it was time to sleep or time to rise and shine.

Then we decided those markers needed further delineation and we made up hours.

Then minutes.

Then seconds.

Now we tick time off in fractions thereof: microseconds, and nanoseconds.[1] Our digitized, computerized, speed-mad world streams by 24/7 at warp speed—or, at least at information transfer rates of so many kilobits and megabits and gigabits and terabits every second.

The base unit of time in the International System of Units as well as other systems of measurement, we usually think of a second as the simple division of a minute into sixty equal measures; the minute being a previous sexagesimal division of the hour. While seconds have been used to measure and calculate time at least since the time of al-Bīrūnī, the preeminent eleventh-century Persian mathematician and astronomer, it wasn't until much later that the second was formally defined as 1/86,400th of a day.

---

1. There are even infinitesimal divisions of time known as picoseconds, femtoseconds, and attoseconds—measures of time equivalent to one-trillionth, one-quadrillionth, and one-quintillionth of a second respectively.

That definition of a second didn't last very long.

Now the scientific standard of time is measured in atomic terms, by the steady frequency of emitted photons: the antiquated second has been updated to "the duration of 9,192,631,770 beats of the radiation corresponding to the transition between two hyperfine levels of the ground state of the cesium 133 atom at rest at a temperature of 0 on the Kelvin thermodynamic scale."

No wonder we're out of breath.

RUSH HOUR

Cesium-beam atomic clocks can measure time accurately to within trillionths of a second. Or, in context, the time needed for a beam of light travelling at 186,000 miles per second to travel less than the distance equivalent to the thickness of a sheet of paper, a page of a book. When it comes to time, accuracy is absolutely important. Think about the air traffic controller and so many planes speeding through space to the same runway . . . or any navigation, be it by air, land, or sea, or even outer space. Timing is everything. A network of atomic timekeepers and other chronographic instruments circles our planet, constantly monitored and synchronized via signals and satellites circling in turn in the space above the planet into near-perfect, super-precise lockstep with each other. All this circling data is continuously collected and analyzed at the International Bureau of Weights and Measures in Sèvres, France day and night, internationally agreed upon as Coordinated Universal Time—as *the* time—then spun back out into the non-stop spinning world and dials of the watches on our wrists to complete the circle.

Still, the planet spins, tilted on its axis just so, and there is evening and there is day. Twenty-four hours, a pirouette: an arbitrary measure of time we agree to obey.

Except we do not all leap gracefully through space at the same speed: circumference and latitude join us in the dance. Because the earth makes one complete revolution on its axis every twenty-four hours (what we have come to know as a "day") we can calculate the surface speed of the spinning earth as the division of the planet's circumference by the same number of hours. We don't all spin at the same tempo, though, because the circumference of the earth decreases latitude by latitude the closer one gets to either the North or South Pole. New Orleans is a bit more up tempo than Fairbanks, Alaska; revelers in Rio dance faster than their counterparts Down Under. At the equator the circumference of the earth is 40, 070 kilometers, which translates to a surface speed of around 1,670 kilometers, or 1,040 miles, per hour. Some thirty-four degrees north of the equator, Los Angeles, California spins at about 860 miles per hour, about the same speed as Tokushima, Japan or Peshawar, Pakistan. Where I live—just about mid-way between the equator and the North Pole—the planet's rotational speed is slower than that, although considerably faster than, say, Qaanaaq, Greenland, or Kirovsk, Russia—or any other human settlement above the Arctic Circle (where any given day may have as many as twenty-four hours of darkness or daylight depending on the season.)

The trouble is, one complete planetary pirouette in the galactic ballet that is the exquisitely choreographed dance of our twirling orbit around the sun—and by which we've decided to measure time and construct a day—doesn't always equal a day exactly all the time and everywhere. The earth's rotational rate is neither static nor a reliable measure of time. In this age of high-precision timekeeping, navigators and astronomers look elsewhere more and more frequently for the tick-tock accuracy upon which we all depend. Astronomical observation over the last two centuries has revealed that the mean solar day—the time it takes for the planet to make one complete revolution on its axis—is slowly but measurably lengthening. Thus, even the measures of time we have come to know as weeks, months, and years are no longer completely accurate.

That is, if we're all even talking about the same year, following the same calendar.

Which we're not.

YEAR AFTER YEAR

While some of us (religious, or not) follow the standard Gregorian calendar, that record of time measures years in relation to the presumed birth of Jesus Christ, a reckoning of time introduced by Pope Gregory XIII in AD 1582, (AD being an abbreviation of *anno Domini*—or, year of our Lord—a notation of historical time first assigned in the sixth century.) To be fair, Gregory hardly invented the system all on his own. He and the rest of the world had inherited earlier—and far from accurate—versions from both Christian and Roman pontiffs and emperors alike (who, in turn, had inherited even earlier calendars from their predecessors; ancient artifacts suggest that even our Paleolithic ancestors created rudimentary calendars more than six millennia ago based on the changes of the moon.) But by the time Gregory was pope the inaccuracies of earlier calendars were wreaking havoc; they were running either too fast or too slow compared to the true solar year or the actual seasons of the planet. The trouble was that so many timekeepers had conveniently rounded up or down (or even manipulated for political reasons) the number of days it took for the ball of dirt we call home to circle the sun. Some calculated the number to be 364; others 365. The more attentive thought the year to be 365 ¼ days. The actual length of the year is closer to 365 days, 5 hours, 48 minutes and 45 seconds—although even that precise counting of time is neither steady nor static: on average, due to the gradual slowing of the earth's rotation, the year decreases in time about half a second every century.

But seconds can turn into minutes; minutes can become hours, become days. By the time Gregory issued his papal bull "officially" correcting what time it was, the calendar had drifted off course by nearly ten days. Easter was no longer eastering when it was supposed to. (Not to mention Passover was passing over at the wrong time, and the Ramadan fast was running slow.) With a stroke of the pen, the days between October fifth and October fourteenth were eliminated from the year 1582. Widely adopted in Catholic countries, the Gregorian calendar took some time to catch on. Protestants, especially, were suspicious, not least because it meant forfeiting nearly ten days of their lives (and wages) forever. The Pope's calendar was not officially adopted in Britain until sometime in the eighteenth century. Japan waited until the century after that, and Orthodox Russians and China held out until the early- to mid-1900s. The Eastern Orthodox Church still does not follow the Gregorian calendar but one based on a system first devised by the ancient Egyptians.

Previous to the Pope's decree a year had been noted AUC, as *ab urbe condita*—or, from the (symbolic) founding of the city and empire of Rome, in what was then the dominant day-keeper of the time—the Julian calendar—a measurement of time introduced by Julius Caesar, itself an updated iteration of an earlier Roman calendar supposedly introduced by none other than the mythic King Romulus and which consisted of only ten months and lasted only 304 days. While the use of BC, or "before Christ," and AD to identify years eventually superseded the Roman idea of what came before and what came after, those markers have now been widely replaced by the less Christocentric terms BCE and CE, or "before the common era" and "common era" respectively. Though there have been plenty of movements to embrace other demarcations of time throughout history. Some timekeepers, for example, lobbied for the observation of time since the "*Era of the Passion*," with year one dating back to AD 33, the presumed date of Christ's crucifixion and resurrection. Mussolini imposed a new calendar, marked *Era Fascista*, to introduce and document his reign of power. The French Revolution ushered in its own method of keeping track of time, the Calendar of Reason, which lasted just over a decade—at which point the new emperor, Napoleon Bonaparte, abolished it.

Regardless of what abbreviation precedes or follows it, however, the Christian liturgical year traditionally begins not with the first day of January but nearly a month before that with the onset of the season of Advent.[2] At one time Hebrew time was measured "since the destruction of the Temple." According to the influential work of the medieval rabbi philosopher and astronomer Maimonides, though, a year in that tradition can also be noted *anno mundi*—or, the year of the world—abbreviated AM.

Whereas the Gregorian calendar is irretrievably linked to the sun, the Hebrew calendar combines the movements of both the sun and the moon. Each month begins with the new moon and follows the lunar cycle of 29–30 days. Add them up and you get only 354 days, whereas a solar year is at least eleven days longer. To account for the difference, the Jewish calendar occasionally adds a leap month—*Adar*—so as to reconcile the cycles of the sun and the moon. (In leap years there must be two Adars.) All of this calculation is to ensure that Passover remains a springtime festival.

Many non-Christians mark the years gone by since the birth or other significant life event of their own religious leaders. The Hindu calendar, for example, begins with Krishna's return to the "eternal abode," in what would be the year 3102 BCE according to the Gregorian calendar. Islam follows a lunar calendar in which year one—marking the year the Prophet Muhammad travelled from Mecca to Medina, and being the equivalent of 622 CE—is noted with the abbreviation AH, Latin for *anno hegirae*—or, year of the migration. The Maya, Aztec, and other Mesoamerican peoples created a great and cyclical calendar system that was far more accurate than the Roman Julian calendar the Spanish conquistadors brought with them

---

2. That there is a Christian liturgical year at all is a notable development in time. The earliest Christians had no use for keeping track of or predicting time, for they understandably believed in the *imminent* return of their Teacher. Human time was seen as an enslaving and worthless thing of this world that kept one's mind attuned to earthly matters rather than the heavenly world to come.

to the so-called "New World." The Chinese calendar began long before the Gregorian one, as did the luni-solar Hebrew calendar.

Still, none of these calendars are precise. Sometimes time doesn't just drift; years have to leap in order to keep up. Nothing stands still.

(I don't know about you, but none of this really makes any sense to me—or, at least it makes about as much sense as the concept of eternity, of something that is more than just time that goes on forever, a measure of time that is somehow beyond time. I can only say, with Emily Dickinson, "On the subjects of which we know nothing . . . we both believe and disbelieve a hundred times an hour, which keeps believing nimble."[3] This is not about unadulterated faith or fact as much as it is about mystery and wonder.)

Scientists and mathematicians now routinely add leap seconds as well as leap months and years to our clocks and calendars and time-torn lives. On more than one midnight in recent history supposedly super-precise atomic clocks around the world were momentarily stilled in order to account for the tilt and wobble of the earth's unique rotation. We do not spin at a constant unchanging angle from the sun, but a constantly changing one as we topple through time and space. In winter we tilt a jaunty 23 degrees, 27 minutes away from the sun; in summer we tip that much toward it. Add to this the construct of Daylight Savings Time (the practice of advancing clocks by one hour in spring and adjusting them backward in autumn, thereby seasonally extending daylight hours, albeit at the expense of the actual time of sunrise and sunset) or where we decide to draw the line between one domestic or international time zone and the next, and the reality is we have no idea what we're really talking about when we say it is whenever-o'clock. We may tend to take both the clock and the calendar for granted, but the truth is we made up yesterday and dreamed up tomorrow. Time as we know it is our own creation, an inheritance of conquest, political order, regulation, and subjugation.

DANCING WITH THE STARS

In time, physicists and mathematicians eventually figured out that everything that really matters—space, us, and time—has to do with light, specifically how ridiculously fast it travels. In the near vacuum of space the speed at which a beam of light travels has been officially defined as 299,792,458

---

3. In Lundin, *Emily Dickinson and the Art of Belief*, 140.

meters per second, usually rounded off to 300,000 kilometers, which translates to just over 186,000 miles per second. (Multiply the speed of light by sixty for the seconds in every minute, another sixty for the number of minutes in an hour, then twenty-four for the hours in a day, and finally 365 for the days in a year and you have a light-year, a unit of measure that reflects the sheer velocity of light and the mind-boggling and incomprehensibly vast distances of space.) Given that enormous scale, the past and the future truly are, as Plato said, merely "created species of time." The only moment in time we can be certain of is this one. All we really have is right now, this fleeting moment that just now whizzed by. We say time flies. But it is really our lives that take wing.

We've been chasing after time's winged chariot ever since time began, talking time management as if we could control the motions of the sun and the moon and the stars, master time, or harness a single hour. Time, it has been said, is what keeps everything from happening all at once. Someone also once said time is just one damn thing after another. Thank God for the last minute—otherwise, nothing would ever get done. Time management theories have come and gone ever since Benjamin Franklin declared time was money in 1748, or even a Shakespearean king lamented, "I wasted time, and now doth time waste me . . ." if not before.[4] To be sure, the rhetoric of time management appeals—all ease, efficiency, and flow:

- The better you control time, the better your life
- Never put off until tomorrow what you can do today (another Franklin-ism) —*and*—
- It doesn't matter if time flies; we're the pilot.

As with night and with day, the words we choose to talk about time reflect our innermost feelings. We are constantly spread too thin. Every day we join the rat race at a breakneck pace. Week after week we return to the same old daily grind, the inevitable treadmill—keeping our nose to the grindstone, our shoulder to the wheel—supervised the whole time by "one-minute managers." We have fast-food and drive-through windows for every possible transaction. Nothing is for here anymore; everything is to go and on the go, and still we hurry up and wait. We've come up with time-saving inventions, like computers and microwave ovens, only to end up

---

4. Shakespeare, *Richard II*, V.v.49., in *The Complete Works*, 466.

impatiently tapping our fingers and feet in front of them as they take mere seconds to perform their assigned duties:

"C'mon, c'mon . . . I don't have all day," we exclaim.

"Take it easy, people!" the actual rats shout from the sidelines.

No matter how hard we try to win the race, we always seem to end up chasing after our own tails. We say there's never enough time in the day. After all, there are only twenty-four hours in each one, right? Unless of course you live on Mars where you'd get almost an extra hour in your day; avoid Jupiter and Saturn, though, whose daily rotation is faster and therefore the days are only ten "hours" long. If you're looking for more time in the day you should really consider Pluto, whether or not it is a planet: it takes more than six days to turn upon itself—a day with well more than a hundred hours in it! The Venusian day is actually longer than its year: Venus makes a complete circuit around the sun every 225 days, but takes 243 days to revolve once around its own axis. I imagine twilight there would be quite spectacular, or at least greatly anticipated, arriving but twice each year.

It's all relative.

When was the last time you thought to yourself, "I have all the time in the world," or someone told you, "take your time"? Everything these days is needed right this instant, PDQ, pronto, ASAP, or at the very least by end of day. We're over-worked, over-extended, and overwhelmed. We live in a world that looks very much like the one Alice discovers in her adventures beyond the looking-glass, one where "it takes all the running you can do to keep in place," and "if you want to get somewhere else you must run at least twice as fast as that."[5]

Our constant prayer: just one more minute, a little more time.

Our own earthly days haven't always been twenty-four hours long, nor will they always be; they were even shorter in the ancient past and will slowly but surely lengthen in the distant future. It's difficult imagine a six-hour-day, struggling as we do to get everything done in the twenty-four we now have, but that is in fact what many scientists estimate the daily spin of the earth was in its infancy. The reason has to do with the moon (amongst other factors) and its spinning dance around us.

In the beginning—or almost the beginning—was the moon and its tidal pull.

If the moon had not joined us on the cosmic dance floor so many eons ago, we would have a very different view of time indeed. Without the moon

---

5. Carroll, *Alice's Adventures in Wonderland*, 136.

there would be no tides to create the friction that slowly but surely slowed our planet from its original spinning speed and our days would whiz by even faster than they do now.[6] Despite the clutch and cling of gravity, though, the moon is slowly drifting away from us, maybe even as much (or as little, depending on your perspective) as an inch or two each year. Concurrently, a second or two is added to our day every several thousand years or so. Nevertheless, at that rate our future descendants will someday look up at an even more distant moon and wonder how we ever got by with only twenty-four hours; their day a hundred-million years from now will be twenty-*five* hours long—or longer.

We say, "Go fast, or be last." We say, "You snooze, you lose." We say, "if only we had the time." The truth is: we *don't*. We do not twirl through time gracefully on our tip-toes like a ballet dancer swept up in the dance, but blunder through it like ogres tripping over our own two left feet and stepping on each other's. The clock is not our savior, not the realization of time but its opposite: the betrayal of time. There's a difference between the merciless hours of the clock and our lives unfolding in time.

There's a reason why methamphetamine (along with other narcotics) is called "speed" and why speed limits are posted on our highways and byways. Still, it seems we're addicted to acceleration, to going faster and faster. The tragic results of spending so much time rushing around at such a soul-blistering pace so focused on the next task, the next thing, the next appointment, the next response to the latest e-mail or text message, is that we completely miss out on the present moment—the one we should be in yet seldom are. Thomas Merton categorized the rush and hurry and overall busyness of the modern workaday world as a kind of violence. The Chinese character for "busy" combines two others: heart, and murder. Still, we're so busy "managing" our time there's no time for anything else.

Forget about thinking. Or prayer.

Eternity will just have to wait. Heaven forfend we pause to admire the way the sun and the moon arc across the sky above us, or how the vesper light glimmers in the gloaming.

Or, to use more scriptural language, to be still and know: "Be still, and know that I am your God" (Ps 46:10).

To simply be.

Still, some worldly metronome bids us dance.

---

6. For more on the moon's role in the length of the terrestrial day, see Comins, *What If the Moon Didn't Exist?*

Stopping isn't really an option; stillness is only an illusion. The very ground beneath our feet is always spinning, as are we along with it, albeit so fast we don't even realize we're moving. And while the planet spins it also orbits—along with our fellow planets—the sun, which in turn revolves around some unknown still point at the center of the Milky Way, a whirling whirligig spiraling ever outward and through space and time ever since the whole shebang began. These days, if we take any notice of twilight whatsoever it is more often than not simply a mindless passing reminder to turn on our headlights at either end of the day's commute, caught up instead in the rushlight of bumper-to-bumper traffic as each of us hurries one way or the other on the workaday expressway to whatever come's next.

And we're running late.

That is to say, if the twilight is even observable, noticeable. Time and the bell no longer bury the day. We've done a pretty good job obliterating it with a constant halogen glare.

NIGHT AND DAY

We run our non-stop lives these days desperately trying to stay one tick ahead of the clock no matter what o'clock it is. In fact, we even go so far as to favor tick over tock in the ticking time-bomb that occupies our every day. And if we can't see what we're doing because it is midnight, we simply banish the dark with a simple flick of a switch.

In the beginning there was light and the light was good. But perhaps there can be too much of a good thing. It seems we've grown accustomed to a different kind of light; we deny the dark, and artificially illuminate it. While we may have solved the problem of the darkness of night, attacking it non-stop with an array of various incandescence, when it comes to getting along with each other we're pretty much still in the dark. "We grow accustomed to the dark," wrote Emily Dickinson, "When light is put away."[7] The dark she referred to was not only the physical night: she penned that line in the midst of one of her country's darkest hours—the American Civil War. Dark times have never been nor ever will be rare occurrences in the history of humankind.

Light might travel at—well, at the speed of light, but wherever it rushes off to so quickly the dark always seems to be there already. We may be able to calculate the speed of light, but what about the parameters of darkness?

7. Dickinson, *Selected Poems*, 57.

If darkness is only an absence, as the scientific-minded assert, then perhaps there isn't anything to calculate. Except we know from experience that darkness isn't merely a lack of light but can also be a palpable force and, at times, all too real.

But then again, maybe the line between light and dark isn't as discrete as we'd like to think. Spend just a few moments on either end of the day watching the sun rise or set and this becomes quite clear. We tell each other that darkness is darkness and light is light, but things aren't really that black and white. The light of each day does not arrive or depart suddenly, but gradually, as we turn toward or away from it.

The planet spins, tilted on its axis just so.

And there is evening and there is day.

And "the event that from the side of the world is called turning . . . is called from God's side redemption."[8]

---

8. Buber, *I and Thou*, 120.

Ordinary Time

We talk about "keeping" time, yet whenever we try to grab hold of it time always seems to evade not just our outstretched hands but also our wondering, wandering minds. Inevitably either time flies . . . or our attention does. While we move through time every day, our mundane lives in ordinary time are neither. Time and again the most brilliant minds over the centuries have tried to explain the enigma of time: when it began and when it will end (if it ever begins or ends); how it passes (if it passes at all); and why it even is—and all have failed. "What is time?" Saint Augustine wondered so very long ago: "Who even in thought can comprehend it?" he lamented. "If no one asks of me, I know; if I wish to explain to him who asks, I know not."[1] At the heart of his spiritual autobiography ticks the notion that if time is where our individual lives unfold, then it is within time here and now that we must find meaning in our lives, or not at all. He believed eternity is our true destination and, like the seventeenth-century Japanese poet Bashō, understood that the journeying itself was a kind of already abiding there. That we, in fact, live in eternity whenever we pay attention to each moment—a thinking not unlike Heschel's exhortation that the timeless lies within the temporal, and what in the practice of Buddhism might be called mindfulness.

"Every day is a journey, and the journey itself is home."[2]

Regrettably, much of Christianity has lost track of Augustine's kind of temporal mysticism and the notion that heaven is accessible within every moment. Eternity is now more often than not thought of as something beyond or above or after; seldom as being somewhere here and now. Certainly ages of astronomers have found no evidence of heaven in the starry

---

1. Augustine, *The Confessions*, 215.
2. Bashō, *Narrow Road to the Interior*, 3.

firmament. The bewildering, puzzling conundrum of time, however, remains. Indelible, untellable time: We are intimately aware of its arrival and departure—indeed, its centrality to our very existence—yet cannot begin to pinpoint its present whereabouts. No matter how quickly and earnestly we try to be present "in the moment," the present moment is already well on its way into the past long before we can ever hope to abide in it. There are days when we feel as if we slog through time and the hours stand still, and others when time slips away before we even realize it was ever here. Time means little to us when we are young; there's little else more important at the prospect of our last days.

We can say, right down to the most infinitesimal division, what time it is. We just can't say what time itself is.

The ancient Greek philosophers all took their turn at cracking the code of time, from Heraclitus's notion that we cannot step into the same river of time twice, to Zeno's definition of time as a series of fleeting moments we call "now" and his resulting question of whether or not we can even say that now, being so transitory, really exists. Plato and Aristotle both paid considerable attention to the question of time and its relationship to eternity. The thinking of Alexander of Aphrodisius—namely, that what we consider to be the past, present, and future is actually an inseparable unity—greatly influenced Saint Augustine's later thoughts about the intrinsically human experiences of memory, attention, and expectation.

Later still, the philosopher Heidegger questioned the idea of a calculable sequence of "nows" and suggested instead a more ecstatic, transcendent nature to time—whether past, present, or future. Accordingly, he also transformed time and space from our usual understanding of them as nouns into verbs—"Of time it may be said: time times. Of space it may be said: space spaces"—and then insisted that in the action of their timing and spacing they hold out to us a unity of what he called "the has-been, presence, and the present that is waiting for our encounter and is normally called the future."[3]

Einstein may have replaced our old concepts of absolute time with one in which time depends upon the position of the observer in space, but we still struggle to let go of our outdated ways of thinking and embrace the implications of such relativity. Indeed, time seems inexplicably and inextricably bound to space for us. We cannot imagine a now not of this created place, for not only are we temporal beings, we are physical creatures: we've

---

3. Heidegger, *On the Way to Language*, 106.

only ever known space in time and experienced time in space. We came from somewhere once upon a time and hope to end up somewhere else sooner or later. Yet if space is infinite—as we hypothesize it is—and we may be at any point in space, it then follows that if time is eternal we may be at any point in time.

Which just doesn't match up with our lived experience of life and death.

It has always been this dual nature of time and eternity, the reality of our numbered hours here and now and the possibility of limitless time elsewhere, which has left us riven and wondering. Perhaps the enigma of time is just too complex for our logical brains and our preference for the precise either/or categorizations of "before" or "after," the discrete distinction between "here and now" and "then and there." This may be why we invented myth and story, ways of getting at truths that we cannot reach via physics or philosophy.

STORY TIME

In the beginning has always been the story, the legend, the tell-told tale. What our ancestors have always understood is that myth is the opposite of neither history nor science but a sacred way of knowing. Long before we ever learned how to read or write we gathered around the campfire or night lantern, the stars twinkling above us, to tell and sing and listen and wonder. We've always relied on the supremacy of story over science, always explained the inexplicable by telling tales, and always turned to once upon a time to explain the always, the already, and the not yet. We tend to associate myth with fiction, fallacy, and falsehood today but, time was, myth provided a secure and sacred container for all we either feared or held dear. Fiction wasn't always (and need not be) perceived as the opposite of scientific fact. Myth and legend have long meted out meaning and mitigated meaninglessness for us; story and song have always been an ancient and necessary manner of communication.

In fact, the language of parable and metaphor is the only vocabulary we really have for whatever came before "in the beginning" and whatever will come after "the end." Free from the constraints of logic and the weight of fact, stories can refer to a time which was beyond time and realities beyond our conceptions of reality.

The story never gets old.

Time, Twilight, and Eternity

Perhaps because we can never really know anything absolute about the origins of time, it has become the very genesis of all our stories. We have no use for the void of uncertainty and chaos. What we want is stability, order, and enduring truths. In one way or another all of the great religions allude to some primordial and temporal beginning. The opening verses of the Hebrew Bible may well be the most widely translated—and wildly debated—example of truth told and understood in terms of parable and narrative. But they're not the only ones. For every once upon a time there is always once upon another time.

For the ancient Greeks time was a hungry god; it devoured life. Yet everything in existence existed in time. All new life arrived and departed not only in space but also in time. To explain this life-giving and life-taking duality they turned to mythology and their pantheon of many deities. Among the first offspring of the primordial Gaia (or Earth herself) and the sky god Ouranos were the Titans, and the youngest among these was Cronus. But Gaia and Ouranos also had other children, horrid creatures with multiple heads and hands, and Ouranos banished them—an act for which Gaia never forgave him. Indeed, she plotted her revenge and called on her children the Titans for help. Only Cronus obliged his mother's request: one night he crept into his parents' bedchamber and castrated his father with a flint blade. The wounded sky god cursed his son and prophesied that one day Cronus would in turn be overthrown by his own son. Eventually, Cronus married another Titan, or Titaness to be exact: his sister Rhea. Together they had many children. But, remembering his father's prophesy, he swallowed each one whole as soon as it was born. Needless to say, this did not please Rhea. The next time she became pregnant she fled to the mountains and secretly gave birth there to none other than Zeus, who would later force his father to regurgitate his siblings, and then lead them in a fierce battle against Cronus and the other Titans, and, yes, overthrow his father and live on in immortality.

The rest, as they say, is history.

As over the top as this timeless myth sounds today it does effectively portray the dual nature of time: life-giving and life-taking, beneficent and monstrous at once. Cronus first begat his children before he swallowed them whole; time first brings life into the world and sustains it before it ultimately takes life away. While Cronus may seem ancient and archaic, his story still reverberates today in the timely words we derived from just one of the words the Greeks had for ordinary time—*chronos*—like chronicle, chronological, or even anachronism and synchronicity. His neutering blade reappears every New Year's Eve as the harvesting scythe carried by the figure of Father Time, or in every personification of death as the Grim Reaper.

Eventually, the Greeks both divided up and multiplied time, as well as its deities. Cronus, originally a symbol of fertility and harvest, became synonymous with an earlier and nearly homophonic personification of time, Chronos, a primordial being responsible in part for the creation of the cosmos. The deity Aion represented eternity, yet another facet of time. The more destructive life-taking aspect of time—the kind of time we fear: ordinary, everyday life passing us by every day—became associated with Cronus. Moments that seemed full of life-giving possibility, however, were embodied by Kairos, or the winged god Opportunity. This is the kind of sacred time that was referred to centuries later in the New Testament. When Mark sat down to record his version of the life and teachings of Jesus Christ, he recorded it in Greek. In his gospel Jesus is reported to have said, "The time has come . . . The kingdom of God has come near" (Mark 1:15). The Greek word for time Mark used in that passage was not *chronos* but *kairos*. In other words, ordinary time had not come and passed by, but a sacred and opportune moment in eternity in which we might fulfill our potential in and with God had arrived.

While *chronos* implied duration and referred to minutes of measured time, *kairos* hinted at wholeness and announced a most meaningful moment. Bound to time and space as much as we are today, what the ancient Greek mind and vocabulary comfortably embodied is that there are many different aspects of and dimensions to time—sequential, celestial, sacred, profane, ordinary, extraordinary—and in order to enter into eternity we must leave behind all our constricting notions of earthly time where both the tiny hummingbird is propelled by wings that flap fifty times per second and the ageless drift of entire continents slowly but surely moves the very ground beneath our feet.

Ordinary, extraordinary time.

The sun does not actually set; it is not gone once it dips below the horizon. Life-devouring time does not win: Zeus defeated Cronus and achieved immortality; the Buddha revealed the dharma, or way, where there is no coming and going, only attentive wakefulness; Lao Tzu said that there are no words for that way—that mystery—that that which is eternal cannot be spoken of, since it lies within; Krishna said that the true Self is changeless and indestructible; Christ was crucified, buried, and rose again—rises still—and said that we will too. All these lived and died in a *then* and *there*, yet somehow remain *here* and *now* with us today.

STILL, IT MOVES

In 1633 Galileo Galilei was brought before the Roman Inquisition under charges of heresy. His crime: promoting heliocentrism, the heretical idea that it was not the sun that circled the earth but the other way 'round—that the earth moved around an immovable sun. The story goes that after officially recanting, and as he left the courtroom for an indefinite imprisonment, the revolutionary thinker defiantly said: *E pur si muove!*—"Still, it moves." He was speaking of the planet we now know is still moving beneath our feet and around the sun, but his words (whether or not he actually said them) also apply to how we experience that movement—that is, by the apparent arrival and departure of time. We may think time is a river flowing in one direction only, or even a series of connected yet distinctly different moments. Still, it moves (as do we). And throughout history time's movement has more often been thought to be as circular as the way in which the sun and the planets appeared to circle around us, or the seasons that go 'round and 'round.

Almost all of the great cultures throughout history have viewed time as circular, revolving, recurrently renewing itself, and utterly eternal—or in a word: cyclical. From the ancient Greeks and Babylonians to the Stoics, to the Hindus and Buddhists in the East, and even the Mesoamerican cultures of the West, time has always gone 'round and 'round again. Aristotle thought about time as cyclical in character, without a beginning or an end, as did Plato. Time has always been a sacred circle or hoop to many indigenous peoples. The Lakota Sioux, for example, noted the changes in where and when the sun rose and set around the horizon during the course of the seasons and thus defined their year as the circle the sun makes around the border of the world. Circular arrangements of stones and other materials were, and still are used in many native ceremonies marking time. The Oglala Sioux leader Hehaka Sapa, also known as Black Elk, wrote of the circular nature of time and the universe:

> Everything the Power of the World does is done in a circle.... The Wind, in its greatest power, whirls. Birds make their nests in circles, for theirs is the same religion as ours. The Sun comes forth and goes down again in a circle. The moon does the same, and both are round.... Even the seasons form a great circle in their changing, and always come back again to where they were. The life of a man is a circle from childhood to childhood and so it is in everything where power moves.[4]

Conversely, time seems to travel like an arrow straight through the Hebrew Bible and the New Testament, an irreversible line of singular events unfolding in an orderly fashion from a point in the past to a hoped-for future—from Genesis to Revelation. But one could also say that the recurrent cycle of night turning to day and circling back to night again is at the very heart of the Bible. The dependable revolution of the sun and the certain cycle of the seasons also circle its pages. The book of Ecclesiastes is fairly dizzy with references to spinning, cyclical time and how everything eventually comes 'round again:

> The sun rises and the sun sets, and hurries back to where it rises. The wind blows to the south and turns to the north; round and round it goes, ever returning on its course. All streams flow into the sea, yet the sea is never full. To the place the streams come from, there they return again.... What has been will be again, what has been done will be done again; there is nothing new under the sun" (Eccl 1: 5–7, 9).

Even the New Testament isn't entirely new or linear: much of what is written about Jesus circles back to Old Testament prophesy, especially from the book of Isaiah. The river of the water of life in the Apocalypse of John (Rev 22:1), is meant to call to mind the primordial river that flowed out from Eden in the first book of the Hebrew Bible (Gen 2:10–14)—from Revelation to Genesis. Revolution seems to be the natural order of creation. The Hindu scriptures teach that time does not begin or end but moves in incredibly long *kalpas*, or cycles of creation and re-creation, like wheels within wheels, each lasting millions of years. For Buddhists, the goal of Nirvana, or liberation, lies beyond the ceaselessly turning Wheel of Existence. "The cycle which includes our coming and going has no discernible beginning

---

4. Cited in Abram, *The Spell of the Sensuous*, 186.

Time, Twilight, and Eternity

or end," wrote the author of the classic Persian poem, the *Ruba'iyat of Omar Khayyam*.[5]

And 'round and 'round it goes . . . The cycle, the circle, the hoop, the wheel—surely none of these round ways of thinking about time are accidental.

The planet spins—tilted on its axis just so—and there is night and there is day.

Yet there was only one Krishna in time and space, just as surely as there was only one Buddha, and one Lao Tzu. There was only one Adam, one Abraham, one Moses who led his people to the Promised Land; only one Jesus who was hung on a cross and who left an empty tomb behind; and just as surely, only one prophet Muhammad to whom God revealed the teachings of the Holy Qur'an. Peace be upon all of them.

There was only one Rumi, one Bashō; only one Vincent van Gogh.

There was only one Galileo.

And there is only one of you and one me, and so far as we know we each have only one life to live. How can we even begin to speak about this life, about birth and growth and death, without acknowledging that there is an inexorably linear direction it appears we all must follow? It's the hereafter we're after here, and always has been—or at least an assurance that it awaits us somewhere and at some point in time. The steady staccato of the ticking clock reminds us, its face objectively observing the events of every moment with complete equanimity and disinterest regardless of whether the moment at hand is trivial or unlike any other in our lives.

Nothing stands still—especially time.

Begin anywhere.

Our greatest pain has always been linked to our notion of coming and going, of taking leave. Both ancient and contemporary teachings have attempted to point out the fault in our thinking. Our birth and death, beginning and ending, are only doors through which we pass, according to one Buddhist sutra, sacred thresholds on our journey through eternity.[6]

More than a century-and-a-half has passed us by since Charles Darwin's theory of evolution made us question human time, that our perspective of time was just that: a construct of our own minds, when—in the greater picture—our time here and now has been only the slightest drop in

---

5. Omar Khayyam, *The Ruba'iyat*, 39.

6. A sentiment expressed in the *Anguttara Nikaya*, the sutra to be administered to the dying. See Hanh, *No Death, No Fear*, xii and 12.

a vast ocean of eons and eras. Earth and the cosmos existed long before us and everything is quite capable of continuing on without us. Regardless of whether or not we find comfort in this scientific revelation, when the sun sets each evening we at least no longer fear the end of the world. An eclipse is no longer an evil portent or bad omen, merely a measurable and predictable phenomenon, albeit a spectacular one. We have made visible things that our predecessors in time only dreamed of seeing; we know things today that were once unknown and mysterious. And yet we still struggle to come to terms with the same merciless fact: while space and time may be infinite we are not. We are finite beings that inhabit material and mortal bodies. Moreover, we are transient, ephemeral creatures both aware of our mortality and at the same time capable of imagining an existence beyond space and time, the possibility that there will be a "who" who will still be after and beyond everything we think we know about who we are now and once were.

It has been nearly four hundred years since Galileo tinkered with the crude spyglasses of his time and first laid eyes on the miraculous spectacles of far-off space that would convince him it was the earth and not the sun that moved. What would that hero of human curiosity make of the powerful telescopes and science of today, I wonder? Or, that a spacecraft named after him might one day be lofted into space, slingshot-swung by the gravity of the moving, spinning earth across the dark universe on a six-year voyage to Jupiter—photographing his planetary home from space all along the way—and ultimately launch its own probe, parachuting it through the Jovian atmosphere, collecting and transmitting data and photographs of that giant planet we now know is awash and aswirl with color as if bathed in the most spectacular sunset?

The moments of our time-bound lives unfold in three-dimensional space. Sometimes time is thought of as a kind of fourth dimension. Yet, as even the slightest consideration of time reveals, time can travel in many directions and has multiple dimensions. We usually limit ourselves to the hourly chime of the clock, the turning pages of a calendar. But we know those are not the only dimensions of time. In fact, we could easily transpose Descartes's famous dictum—*cogito ergo sum*, "I think; therefore I am"—and say *tempus agito ergo sumus*, "time moves; therefore we are."

Still, it moves.

Unless it doesn't—and *we* are what moves through *it*.

"The events in our lives happen in a sequence in time," wrote the novelist Eudora Welty, "but in their significance to ourselves they find their own order, a timetable not necessarily—perhaps not possibly—chronological. The time as we know it subjectively is often the chronology that stories and novels follow: it is the continuous thread of revelation."[7]

So which is it, then, river or round; a circle of time or an unbending line? Here we are again back at either/or, when what we really need is an image that captures the multi-directional flow of time, both cyclical and linear at once. Something perhaps more like a Mobius strip as it twists and curves through space which, if we could travel its length we would always return to our starting point having traversed both sides of its entire length without ever crossing any edge or boundary at all.

Millennia after an evangelist recorded in Greek the Aramaic words of a Jewish rabble-rouser, or further the ancient Greeks divided time between the profane and the sacred, between *chronos* and *kairos*, an ecumenical and anonymous group of South African theologians sat down in 1985 to write what would become a catalyst for momentous and long-awaited change in the politics and government of that country—specifically an end to the apartheid regime. They titled their challenge to the church and country "The Kairos Document."[8] No ordinary measure of time, but rather a moment of action and truth had arrived in Soweto, one that would sweep across the nation and the world—and take apartheid with it once and for all, altering forever the history and fate of so many human lives.

Ultimately, the important question isn't whether time is a flat line of uniquely unrepeatable and sequential moments or a part of some vast revolution of mystery—that is, the difference between chronology and synchronicity. That certainly isn't the only question. Perhaps a more interesting inquiry would be whether or not now is all there really is, all we're meant for? Or, if eternity exists just where is it and how and when might we get there: here or elsewhere . . . before or after? Are our lives meant to be sacrificial or sacramental? Are we better than our worst moments, or is life merely a merciless accumulation of yesterdays?

---

7. Welty, *One Writer's Beginnings*, 68–69.

8. Writing at a volatile time and at great risk to their personal safety, the authorship of the letter remains somewhat unclear. When it was eventually published its authors were simply listed as "Kairos Theologians." See *The Kairos Document*.

Ordinary Time

By any perspective the real question is one of stewardship over dominion, and whether we view each and every moment we have here together as ordinary or extraordinary.

Already/Not Yet

Time is a doorway through which we are always departing and arriving; every moment is a threshold we cross. Our days and nights and seasons and lives are filled with such passages, but one of the most beautiful thresholds we experience is the twice daily transformation of night into day and day into night: twilight. The dusk and the dawn are both liminal threshold times where lightness and darkness mingle; go-betweens between one day and the next where one day is not yet done and another not yet begun; hinges of time on which night and day turn. Both neither/nor zones of ambiguity and in-betweenness; temporal embodiments of both/and.

The metaphor has always held open the space between. The ancient Celts saw the threshold as a meeting point between heaven and earth; the poetry of the Sufi mystic Rumi is full of doorways between our hearts and to the beloved. Similarly, Krishnamurti spoke of "opening the window" between one's true self and the divine. Jesus crossed threshold after threshold, the New Testament tell us, even when the doors appeared to be closed shut. According to at least one translation of the Hebrew Psalms, morning and evening are both "gateway" moments when God's creation sings (Ps 65:8, NRSV).

Begin with a doorway in time, then. Begin with a blue hour, a saffron dawn, a pink moment . . . an impossibly golden and purple sunset. An interstitial space that holds the edges of night and day—and everything we know—together: both a border and meeting point, margin and middle at once; a simultaneous separation and connection.

In nature this temporal frontier is called crepuscular, a word that refers to anything most active during the marginal hours, the twice daily edges of night and day, the twilit time when the changeover from diurnal to nocturnal activity occurs. We slow down, while other creatures start up. Beauty does not belong only to the light. Proof:

- moonflowers and angel's trumpets scenting the evening air
- the eye-shine of the deer that browse in the hedgerow
- the fluorescent flicker of the fireflies as they mate in the meadow
- the flutter and dart of the little brown bat
- the haunting call of the woodcock
- or the distinctly nonhuman screech we explain away as hoot of owl

Of the crepuscular there are even two varieties: the vespertine, active only at dusk; and the matutinal, or matinal, active only at dawn.

But even in these crepuscular moments we often seem to favor the dawn over dusk—bright light over opaque dark—the hope and promise of a new beginning at the dawn of a new day over the perceived ending that awaits on the other side of every sunset. The dawn in our minds represents the beginning of a new day full of new possibilities, while in our heads we've demonized dusk into the embodiment of uncertainty: all lurking shadows and things that go bump in the night. We do the same to the seasons too, equating spring and summer to birth, growth, and our younger natures; while autumn we associate with the harvest of middle and old age, and our wintery deaths waiting just after. (When in reality, at least for those living in the northern hemisphere, the dark days and long nights of winter do not signal the end of a year but a new beginning.) We think the day-flying butterfly beautiful; the nocturnal moth is a messenger from the land of the shadows. The diurnal dove descends from heaven; the nighttime bat has demon wings and flies like—well, like a bat of hell.

Begin with our diurnal nature attempting to make sense of the approaching dark and its nocturnal creatures. With binary thinking and either/or; with night *or* day, with light *or* dark.

NEITHER/NOR

The pink moment, as sunset is sometimes called, is a queer one; no other hour of the day is quite like it. All atmosphere, with foundation and attitude—and throwing a little bit of shade—Twilight is a beautiful drag queen, a convincing illusion of paint and color, glitter and glam, of both/and—and everything in between. But twilight, like drag, is not about masquerading as something else, nor simply a spectacular spectacle. It is not night pretending to be day or night, but transcendence embodying its transcendent self.

Time, Twilight, and Eternity

An is-ness we not only witness but with which we inter-are. By day the blue sky is all business; by night its dark dome bids us rest. But in between it tucks all that away and slides into something a little more colorful, wonderful, fabulous . . .

Divine.

"I think it pisses God off if you walk by the color purple in a field somewhere and don't notice it," one of the characters says in a line that gives Alice Walker's epic novel, *The Color Purple*, its title. "People think pleasing God is all God cares about. But any fool living in the world can see [God is] always trying to please us back."[1] What takes our breath away and makes us stop and take notice in the first place is the sheer beauty of any sunrise or sunset—or at least, it should. Dusk and dawn are not only luminous but numinous: mystical moments in the cycle of our days when the universe breaks open its heart. Instances when and where "the veil of the world is very thin," as the Irish might say, thresholds where the sacred can be seen and the holy can seemingly seep through, almost imperceptibly.

In the beginning—at least for the ancient Greeks—was beauty: the unifying and creative force that bestirs the world. For them there was a distinct difference between the "beautiful" and "beauty" itself. The former described whatever participated in beauty; the latter, whatever made things beautiful in the first place, its source—beauty not only in the eye of the beholder, but also in the act of beholding. To recognize beauty not as something one happened to experience, but as the heart of all life was to see the ultimate sacredness and belonging of every moment and thing. It still is: twilight twice daily offers not only a glimpse of its inherent beauty—its creation and existence—but also a fleeting look at our own belonging as it calls us beyond ourselves. Fixing our gaze on the rising or setting sun can be a supremely spiritual discipline: one of *beholding*.

Beauty captures our attention because so often it seems to arrive from out of nowhere and for no good reason, embodying the sense of timelessness that has always somehow felt like home to us. Yet as luminous and timeless as beauty is, what makes it precious is its transience: Beauty fades, disappears. While the beautiful finds a certain home in the human eye and within us, the eye also shows us that beauty is not within but outside of and beyond us. We do not live in an ever-glowing sunrise or sunset—far from it.

And so we labor on the threshold of presence and absence, time and eternity.

1. Walker, *The Color Purple*, 196.

Already/Not Yet

The French philosopher, political activist, and Christian mystic Simone Weil said that when it comes to the holy and each other (all that really matters, really) paying attention is paramount; that it is the very act of looking that ultimately saves us. And by looking she meant not only searching and paying attention, but also the physical act, the human sense of vision. "Sin is not a distance," she wrote, "it is a turning of our gaze in the wrong direction."[2] Paying attention is the penultimate prayer.

Dusk and dawn are the wild eyes of God. The question is do we dare return the gaze? And if so, just exactly how does one look into the unearthly radiance of God's shining eyes?

(And who knew God loves eye-shadow so much?)

Begin again.

Begin with Plato's dictum: We become what we behold.

"The eye with which I see God is the same eye with which God sees me," Meister Eckhart wrote.[3] We think we see by opening our eyes, the visual organs that reside in the orbital sockets of our skulls. But though we do see the world outside us when we open our eyes, if we depend only on those physical organs we are ultimately short-sighted. It is with our hearts that we truly perceive realness. In addition to the "eye of the flesh" which is capable of sight, early medieval Christian philosophers believed that we also had access to the "eye of reason" as well as the "eye of true understanding." From Saint Augustine's perspective there were distinctly varying forms of vision: outer seeing, the most basic form of seeing by means of the organs of our eyes and which was inadequate when it came to perceiving matters of eternal truth; and inner seeing, which employed the eyes of the soul and intellect. In Hinduism there is *darshan*, the "auspicious sight" of enlightened beings in which both beholding and being beheld take place concurrently.

There are things not visible to the human eye. The millions and millions of optical rods and cones that make up our sense of sight have nothing on the focusing power of the human heart. We can see so much more when we look with more than our eyes—when we allow, for example, our hearts to glance Godward. The contemplative heart is one that sees and functions like a prism; it can split experience into a whole spectrum of truth. Just as pure light passing through a prism breaks into a colorful spectrum—and the ancient light of the universe traveling at a certain angle through time

---

2. Weil, *Waiting for God*, 73.
3. Eckhart, *Sermons and Treatises*, 87.

and the particles and disturbances of our atmosphere produces breathtakingly beautiful skies—so too can our hearts break apart the world we think we see and reveal its most radiant inner reality. That is, if the heart's crystal is clear. Too often we allow the world to smudge and darken the glass, distorting whatever light can emerge. Attention, mindfulness, and prayer, though, can remove the dust and streaks and fingerprints of any life lived. Twice daily twilight crosses over the threshold of space and time and enters our world, and invites us to look ...

And to look again.

Because seeing takes time.

Lingering at the threshold takes a certain patience and willingness to go wherever the moment takes us. But that does not mean we must we leave ourselves behind in order to follow the beauty of any sunrise or sunset. Like any sublime moment in nature, twilight guides us ever inward to our more elemental, reflective nature. Every dusk and dawn can be experienced both exteriorly and interiorly. And in praying within those twilit moments we can be both carried away from and brought ever deeper into the depths of our being. Pause long enough to sense and feel, and not just watch, the ember of the rising or setting sun ascending or descending and it isn't difficult to recognize the numinous in it—to see *Atman*, the flame that the Hindu Upanishads use to describe the soul; or the feared and revered Vedic fire god Agni setting the sky ablaze. Or a reminder of the Buddha's *Āditta Sutta*—his "Fire Sermon": that the fires which illuminate every morning and evening also burn within us. Or to see the flickering flame of the Shabbat candle, an honoring and a remembrance; the burning call of the heart that sets the Sufi dervish spinning and burns away all traces of separation; or even imagine twilight as a glowing host held above the chalice of our day.

Sacraments, all.

That the pupils of the eyes of all animals have the power to increase or diminish according to greater or lesser light has fascinated the curious-minded at least since Leonardo da Vinci recorded his observations on owl's eyes in his scientific journals sometime in the fifteenth century. The eyes of nocturnal creatures contain many more rods than cones, making them more adept at perceiving things like shadow, shape, and movement. But our human eyes with their preponderance of optical cones are made for rejoicing in color, tint, and hue. Who knows what evolutionary purpose it serves for us to be able to recognize the lavender mists and lilac vapors of twilight?

Perhaps beauty isn't merely superfluous but somehow sustains—and the sky, as Emerson wrote, really is "the daily bread of the eyes."[4]

Eyelids flutter open, and light enters in. Nothing could be simpler.

Look, gather in, repeat; it's how we know the world. Or is it? Just looking is not really the same thing as paying attention, seeing, knowing and understanding. Though we seldom just look—more often than not we look for, look forward, look back, look after or around, and of course we constantly overlook. And we look away. All too often our eyes seem to have a will of their own, or are merely spies sent out to gather intelligence by our commanding memories, assumptions, and expectations.

We may be diurnal creatures, but the human eye still possesses a remarkable agility and ability to adjust to darkness. The aperture of our pupils can open wide in order to gather the faintest photons and thereby focus and intensify the vaguest glimmers of illumination available. Even more so can the human heart, an essential organ that is both diurnal and nocturnal.

The heart beats even in the dark.

When we look at twilight through the ocular prism of the heart, we can discover a universe where the darkness and the brightness of our lives dwell together, a universe in which the most meaningful thresholds of life lay open and await our crossing. Twilight is a very real altar in time on which the liturgy of our lives unfolds. It takes our preconceived distinctions and certainties—whether of day and night, light and dark, or life and death—and holds them in connection and conversation with each other (and in that conversation they can be altered themselves.) The gloaming is a holy threshold where not only night mingles with day, and light with dark, but earth with heaven. And we are the focusing lens
—between—

4. Emerson, *The Journals*, VI, 410.

Vespers

Time and Again

I.

Begin with betwixt and between and with both/and.

Whether before or after, or beyond before and after, it is in the middle of time we stand on the threshold of elsewhere and otherwise: an invisible place, a geography of grace. What was, is, and will be. Between the lines of history

—between you and me—

time and eternity:

Where distance is absolved by simple presence, where the known is unlearned and the unknown awaits just out of sight, and stillness propels at the speed of light.

Begin with the already/not-yet of twilight. Begin on the brim and brink; start in the middle that is also somehow the margin—on the edge of, on the verge of . . .

becoming

not yet night; not still day—a gateway, doorway, passageway—

Point of departure and arrival,

origin and completion.

II.

Begin with the daily turn of the planet, with shadow-rise. Begin with umbra and penumbra, with darkening skies.

Let go of the light; let darkness fall.

Begin with evening—a new day.

Time, Twilight, and Eternity

This day.

Begin before night has found its first star. With the sun sinking below the horizon by degrees; a fleeting meeting between day and night where testimony is given—one day to the next, one night to the next. Begin with faint stars emerging seemingly from nowhere and sliding into place—Sirius, Arcturus, Rigel—a moment of in-between; neither light nor dark, here nor there; neither a beginning nor an end.

(Again)

Begin in the dark.

Begin before filaments of tungsten were impossibly coiled and heated white-hot inside thin bubbles of glass; before arcs of electricity ever shot through vapors of mercury; before ballast, electrode, or semi-conductor; before neon, or xenon, or argon—before metal halide.

Begin with the division of space into light and dark, of time into night and day. The hours, a word—twilight—

another: sunset.

Fast falls the eventide. Begin with a hymn sung to the night. First the night, then the light: every dawn, the light—and after the light, night.

(Again)

Begin with revolution...

With the ancient Celts giving thanks to the great Turner of nights and days, the One who makes the seasons go round, who circles and spins dawn to dusk... to dawn again. With the Neolithic farmers who kept track of time by building a circle of standing stones, a temple of light and shadow. Or with the Shakers' simple gift of turning and turning in order to get to the place where we ought to be—to come round right. With a poet dancing at the still point of a turning world, neither forward nor backward. With the medieval definition of God as a circle whose circumference is nowhere and whose center is everywhere; or with Dante's vision of Paradise as a ring of heaven which stills its center and revolves all else. With the Sufi whirling body around heart—around the source of Divine love and grace—as an electron around a nucleus, as a planet around its sun, as the galaxy itself spins.

Begin with prayer: there the dizzying dance begins.

Begin with Saint Francis composing a canticle to the sun and to the moon; with the Buddhist monk reflecting on permanence and reciting mantras to the rising sun, singing sutras to the setting sun. Begin with the call of the muezzin, with the faithful washing their hands and opening their prayer mats and books; with the Muslim performing *ṣalāt al-maġrib*—the fourth prayer of the day—in the gloaming. Or with the elaborate hand gestures and arabesques of the Hindu ritual designed to greet and revere the sun morning, noon, and night.

(Again)

Begin with the Christian monastic praying through time a liturgy of hours, marking the passing day by the length and depth of prayer rather than by the tick of a clock. Keeping track not of time, but of eternity: rising in the middle of the night to perform vigils, then matins or lauds; saying prime at dawn; terce, and sext, and none throughout the day; chanting vespers before the sunset and compline to the starry night.

(Again)

Begin with the devout Jew saying *Ma'ariv*, the evening prayer, by starshine, praying to the One who evenings the evening:

Baruch atah, Adonai, ha-ma'ariv aravim.

Begin with plainsong, with evensong, with common prayer. Begin with ordinary time. Begin with the commonplace, and the everyday grace

of a rising and setting sun.

III.

Begin with nightfall and with another day. Begin with this day, a new day—the only day.

Start where you are.

Begin with reading the sky for the prayers of the hour; with time made holy, a sacred breathing space, with time transformed into temple, cathedral, a holy place—

Time hallowed; time sanctified, consecrated

every day.

Begin with tranquility, with the utility and futility of—stillness. Begin with a wandering mind, a doubtful attitude, and a restless body. Begin with prayer—or, the beginning of prayer: begin with yes, with thank-you.

—Amen.

Begin with holy ground and unshod feet. Begin with gravity, with gratitude, or with whatever brings us to our knees. Begin with time broken open, with hearts broken open.

(Again)

Time, Twilight, and Eternity

Begin with twilight, a suspended hour. Begin with sunset, with starshine, with Sabbath. Begin with continuity and keeping commandments. Remember the Sabbath and keep it holy. Begin with tradition

—*And there was evening, and there was morning: a day*—

Or begin with relativity; not with the horizon of time forming the perimeter of all that we know but with the speed of light, with the universe and everything in it in motion—a timeless having-been that will always be. With the possibility of spinning through space so fast that mass and matter become infinite and time stands still.

Begin with darkness and nothingness . . .

and the improbable possibility of us

being.

Here.

Now.

Night Flowers

With every revolution shadows rise. They stretch and lean and lengthen below evening skies. Rooftop silhouettes intermingle with outlines of trees and mountains and passersby. Streetlamps begin to hum and glow in anticipation. Birds fall silent as they wing their way home to night roosts and nests. Crickets begin to chirp and call; fireflies blink. The sun sets, leaving everything tipped in tinsel and sapphired—first orange, then fuchsia and cerise tinged with lavender frosted gold, and finally, an impossibly roseate indigo—and twilight begins: the dawn of night.

Sunset, night rise; where one ends and the other begins confounds our eyes. As vivid and versicolored as any sunset may be it never pinpoints exactly the end of day. Twilight, however glorious and spectacular its pyrotechnics may be, is never a distinct event but something more subtle: an unfolding. The day departs—night arrives—more like a blossom revealing its petals. And every twilight bouquet is unique and fleeting and temporal, composed of ephemeral blossoms gathered just so and unfolding only *once* in time; every sunrise and sunset a garden of evening primrose and morning glories, night jasmine and day lilies.

The blossoming skies of twilight have always captured the fascination of astronomers and artists, poets and physicists and picnic-goers alike. Think of Monet's lavender haystacks in the varying light, or Vincent van Gogh's paintings of sunset in the garden of the asylum where he ended his life; Chagall's deep blue dreams; Albert Bierstadt's magisterial landscapes of the American West; or even the surprisingly luminous skies of so many of James McNeill Whistler's compositions. (While perhaps known most famously for the portrait of his mother he titled *Arrangement in Grey and Black*, his many "Nocturnes" and the painting *Red and Gold: Salute, Sunset* especially reveal a fascination with the colorful and ever-changing skies of twilight.) Whistler was not alone when he noted the artistic value of "dim dawns and dusks," and how they transfigured even the most commonplace and mean things of life by their "exquisite and evanescent effects." Indeed, the popularity of sunset and sunrise as subject matter for painters in the nineteenth century prompted one critic to note that it was "almost impossible to keep count" of the number of such paintings submitted to at least one 1899 salon.[1]

What any painter would tell you is that in the beginning was color: Light broken open.

For us.

Literature too has long reminded us of the specialness, even the holiness of twilight. Shakespeare's star-crossed lovers would be nowhere without the breaking light of dusk and dawn—the nightingale and the lark—and the poetry of the night.[2] "What is it about this twilight hour?" Izumi Shikibu noted in a love poem penned long before the Bard of Avon ever picked up his quill, "Even the sound of a barely perceptible breeze pierces the heart."[3] Henry David Thoreau saw sunset as a unique moment in the scroll of time, one that offered a peek at Paradise: "Who has not seen in imagination, when looking into the sunset sky, the gardens of the Hesperides, and the foundation of all those fables?" he inquired.[4] (He was referring to the Greek tales of the Hesperides, the daughters or nymphs of Evening, their gardens the Greek counterpart to Eden; an original paradise.) The Welsh poet Henry Vaughan also caught a glimpse of eternity, and our relation to it, in the twilit sky:

> Like a great ring of pure and endless light,
> All calm, as it was bright;
> And round beneath it, Time in hours, days, years,
> Driv'n by the spheres
> Like a vast shadow moved; in which the world
> And all her train were hurled.[5]

---

1. In Thompson, *Monet to Matisse*, 109.

2. E.g., Romeo's famous comparison of Juliet to the eastern light, dawn, and the sun (II.ii.1–32); and the later scene in which the lovers confuse dawn with dusk and the call of the nightingale and the lark (III.v.1–10). See Shakespeare, *Romeo and Juliet*, in *The Complete Works*, 484 and 497, respectively.

3. See Komachi and Shikibu, *The Ink Dark Moon*.

4. Thoreau, *Walking*, 21.

5. In Negri, *Metaphysical Poetry*, 176.

THE MUSIC OF THE SPHERES

In the beginning there was silence.

Then something or someone struck a chord somewhere. Listen carefully and you can still hear strains of that music in the unfolding sky. The philosophical concept of *musica universalis*, or "the music of the spheres" is an ancient melody. While this music was not usually thought of as being physically audible, but rather another form of harmony or mathematics—or even spiritual revelation—it proportionately embodied and intoned the movements of the Sun and Moon and the stars, and ordered the heavens; an idea that fascinated thinkers as early as Pythagoras and flourished until the end of the Renaissance. Medieval thought clearly differentiated between the music of the spheres, the internal music of the human being, and the musical sounds produced by instruments that we tend to think of as "music" today.

Composers have long written ballads to the dusk and the dawn. Esoteric and pedestrian theologies alike continue to place heaven and consciousness squarely within the music of the spheres. Mention sunrise and sunset, and fans of stage and screen alike are apt to break out singing the sentimental soundtrack to *Fiddler on the Roof*. And without the revolving pattern of dawn and dusk, there neither would have been reason for Pete Seeger to set an ancient Hebrew text to music—to everything there is a season (Eccl 3:1–8)—nor an audience to hear The Byrds singing, "Turn! Turn! Turn!" to the topsy-turvy world of the 1960s. Popular music is full of lyrical references to the gloaming (think of The Platters singing "Twilight Time" or Roy Orbison's tender ballad "When the Blue Hour Comes.") But twilight is a classic. Schumann and Mendelssohn both wrote *Abendlied*, or Evening Songs, and Philip Glass composed a more modern setting of yet another. Dvorak heard vesper bells in the sunset sky; Debussy believed there was nothing more musical than a sunset. The South African anti-apartheid leader Nelson Mandela found great pleasure and solace in listening to classical music recordings while watching the sun set beyond the now infamous penitentiary at Robben Island where he was imprisoned.

Notions of finding hope, if not God in nature—if not Nature itself as God—are as old as time itself. If one cannot believe in a personal God, at least there is the lawful and incomprehensibly miraculous hum and harmony of the universe: the music of the spheres. This is neither sacrilegious nor anthropomorphic. We need look no further than Albert Einstein, who saw and heard in nature and the sky above our heads "a magnificent structure that we can comprehend only very imperfectly, and that must fill a thinking person with a feeling of humility . . . a genuinely religious feeling."[6]

TRANSITORY TWILIGHT

While we refer to the daily dip of the sun below the horizon of the spinning planet beneath our feet by many names sunset is, in fact, distinct from both dusk and twilight in the garden of the sky. We say sunset heralds the night, but before there is ever night there is dusk. And in the in-between there is twilight. The sunset sky above us is never a solid field of color—not a garden sown with one variety of seed only—but a riot of night blossoms: sunset, gloaming, eventide, dusk, twilight, evening, afterglow, sundown, vespers, half-light. . . The blue hour doesn't only blow blue: it blooms orchid and rose, buttercup and jonquil, fuchsia and marigold.

Twilight itself has been officially divided into three distinct phases. The U.S. Naval Observatory recognizes civil, nautical, and astronomical twilight. Civil twilight begins right after "sunset" and ends when the center of the sun is six degrees below the horizon, and marks the time when street lamps start to glow and car headlights are usually switched on so that we can safely drive to where we are headed. Approximately a half an hour later, nautical twilight signals when it is dark enough that the brightest stars are visible for navigation purposes. (Although increasingly dark the horizon is still visible during nautical twilight, which allowed—and still allows—for mariners to take accurate sightings between stars or other celestial bodies and the visible horizon in order to keep track of both their location and destination.) Astronomical twilight, the darkest of all the vesper lights, occurs when the center of the sun is a full eighteen degrees below the horizon and marks the beginning of a period of darkness when even the faintest of stars become visible to the naked eye.

It is dusk.

---

[6]. In Dukas and Hoffman, *Albert Einstein*, 39. Einstein's view of the (inter)relationship between science and religion is well documented, even if his idea of "God" was unorthodox. Regarding those who he recognized as not believing in God, he once said "what makes me really angry is that they quote me for support of such views." He also said, "Then there are the fanatical atheists whose intolerance is the same as that of the religious fanatics, and it springs from the same source. They are creatures who can't hear the music of the spheres." For additional insight into Einstein's cosmic view of the world, see Martin and Ott, *The Philosophy of Albert Einstein*.

Night Flowers

The planet spins and there is evening—three twilights—an accumulating darkness; the incrementally fading light of each day going, going . . . Gone.

Except it all depends on how you measure a day; where you mark its beginning and end.

WHEN DOES A DAY BEGIN?

We tend to think of morning as the start of a new day, that our lives unfold as if in a movie or a play: from sunrise to sunset. Or at least we think the day begins with the screech or ring of the alarm clock, whenever it sounds. Physicists and astronomers adhere to a measure of time based on the tropical or mean solar year, which measures a "year" from one vernal equinox to the next and a "day" from noon to noon. Our modern—albeit distinctly Roman in origin—calendar reckons time and days from the middle of one night to the middle of the next, literally from midnight to midnight. Observant Jews and many Sabbatarian Christians, however, begin their holy days long before or after the clock strikes twelve: their days begin with sunset, an echo of a Divine reckoning of time.[7] In fact, in many traditions the day does not end with the arrival of night nor in the middle of it but begins with evening, with sunset. Nighttime does not bring the night but a new day. An ever-unfolding Alpha and Omega, sundown is never simply the end—that is, not until the next sundown . . . at which point yet another day begins.

(Again.)

Every day turns on twilight—twice daily—at dusk and at dawn. And then at dusk again. While easily observed on any given day that does not make twilight mundane or commonplace. Nor should it be taken for granted. On the contrary, its unfolding petals can be a beautiful reminder that the dark and spinning sphere we call home spins neither haphazardly nor aimlessly, but dances in step and tune with some greater order and pattern. We can calculate the hour at which the sun will "rise" or "set," divide twilight into as many stages as we can think of, and yet the beauty of each

---

7. A reckoning based primarily on the creation story as it occurs in the Bible, specifically the line "and there was evening and there was morning—the first day" (Gen 1:5). In addition, there are several other passages in the Hebrew Bible which are often cited as precedents for reckoning the day from sunset or evening, e.g., Lev 23:32; Neh 13:19; Judg 14:18; and the Passover instructions which instruct: "from the evening of the fourteenth day until the evening of the twenty-first day you shall eat unleavened bread" (Exod 12:18).

dawn and dusk remains unpredictable. Never quotidian, twilight is always a surprise, a gift.

The sunset sky can be not only a physical manifestation of optics and physics but also an orientation of the heart; a comfort in the face of the terror we feel all too often in encroaching darkness and perceived endings; a sign that salvation exists—and that after and out of darkness comes light.

Eden, it turns out, doesn't have to be a garden:

In the beginning—and after all—is the paradise of twilight.

Still Life

Imagine just one day when you had absolutely nothing to do: twenty-four hours in which everything you might need was already provided and you need not do anything—no work obligations, no blizzard of text messages or e-mails to respond to, no to-do list to complete, no errands to run—nothing to do but to be. What activities would you need to set aside in order to do that? To drop out of the rat-race for just a few hours and, for once, just "be"?

To be still and know...

Nothing to do but cease, rest, bless, and make holy.

According to the Hebrew Scriptures the One who was there at the beginning of all beginnings did just that: "... so on the seventh day [God] rested from all his work. Then God blessed the seventh day and made it holy, because on it he rested from all the work of creating that he had done" (Gen 2:2b–3).

If God stopped—the first Sabbath day—surely we can.

"Better is one hand full of quietness," according to the Hebrew Scriptures, "than two hands full of toil and a striving after wind" (Eccl 4:6).

Or at least one would think so.

The concept of stopping or even slowing down seems increasingly foreign if not well-nigh impossible in the whirlwind of our busy days and our 'round-the-clock, speed-mad world. Sure, keeping busy can sometimes feel good and, if we're lucky, work can even be fulfilling and rewarding. But there's a reason we also sometimes call the workaday world "the daily grind": it can be utter drudgery, demoralizing, and a deadly drain.

Regardless of whether the thought of stopping appeals to us or appalls, too many of us seem to have forgotten just how to stop. How to leave loose ends untied and what isn't done undone. Especially since as soon as we do what needs to be done a new thing to be done takes its place. Go and do is all it seems we ever do; seldom do we stop and be. We may occasionally figure out a way to take a momentary pause from actual work, but we rarely un-plug completely from the demands of the virtual world that entangles us in its world-wide web. We don't even need a plug to remain plugged in anymore; our work-world is increasingly wireless, hyper-connected, and constantly urging us to multi-task. Our every relationship seems directed by devices these days—and they're not of our own. We are always on, and we're hyper-stressed . . . perhaps because our days consist of one hyperlink after another. Yet, more and more of us report higher and higher levels of anxiety when our so-called smartphones and digital doo-dahs are merely out of our sight.[1]

Don't get me wrong, I'm certainly no Luddite. I cannot imagine writing these words without the wonders of word processing and digital file storage; the miracles of the micro-chip, the hard drive, the laptop computer, or the Internet. If time is money, though, it seems we're always trying to make ends meet even in this world of time-saving technology—and just barely getting by. The digital age has surely been a good and helpful servant. But it is quickly becoming our master. The less tethered, although more connected, we become to technology the less time we seem to have left for anything "real"—time, life, or even each other.

Say nothing about God.

Work means food on the table, a roof overhead, a warm bed to sleep in, and maybe even a sense of identity and self-worth. We spend more of our adult life "on the job" (or getting there) than anywhere else. Yet more and more Americans report they are increasingly cynical about, and unhappy at, work.[2] As numerous as our hours are here on this ceaselessly spinning world there never seems to be enough of them in any day. We dream of "stealing" a moment just for ourselves, as if it were a crime; we talk of "making" time for something or someone, as if we can control the forces of the universe. And when we make it to the end of the work-week we exclaim TGIF, "Thank God It's Friday." (Even though most of us are simply relieved and rarely actually thank God—or Allah, or Buddha—or for that matter, even the universe, or the clock, or whoever dreamed up the five-day work-week to begin with.)

1. A number of articles and books have explored this and other related phenomena related to the digital shift in our information gathering and communication. See, for example, Cheever et al., "Out of Sight," 290–297; and Rosen et al., *iDisorder*.

2. An alarming seventy percent of those surveyed in Gallup, Inc.'s 2013 poll, *State of the American Workplace*.

Still Life

THE GIFT OF TIME

"The day is yours and yours also the night," the poet of the ancient Hebrew Psalms sang to his God (Ps 74:16). Even in the midst of adversity we are not consumed: God's compassion rises anew every morning, the prophet of the Book of Lamentations proclaims (Lam 3:22–23). Our hours themselves are constantly born anew regardless of how we fill them: with work or play, texting or resting, surfing the web or mindful attention. That we are ever able, amidst the relentless rush of time, to pause and ponder or pray is perhaps a wonder, if not a kind of remarkable grace. Regardless, God's first gifts—night and day, the hours—arrive on the horizon blessing after blessing, time and again. The question is whether or not we receive them, carefully unwrap the present. Or do we keep the receipt, the price tag and labels intact, so that we can thanklessly return it? Do we abide in time, or do we bide our time until something better comes along?

"You shall labor and do all your work," the Hebrew Scriptures command, "but the seventh day is a Sabbath to God. On it you shall not do any work . . ." (Exod 20:9–10). Still the planet spins, tilted on its axis just so, and creation continues to unfold. There are all kinds of loose ends yet to be woven into its tapestry. God stopped and rested to bless and make holy even though the work was not completely finished and there was still more to come. More to do.

Shabbat, as the Sabbath is called in Hebrew, like all Jewish days, begins at sunset because in the story of creation it says: "And there was evening, and there was morning, one day" (Gen 1). When we begin with evening we do not begin at the end of anything but with our earliest beginnings and our truest home. The first time the word "holy" is used in the Hebrew Scriptures is at the end of the creation story; the first days were all good, but the seventh day was set apart as *qadosh*, as holy.

Begin with the first week, then, and with the seventh day. Begin with three stars visible in the gloaming and the twilight grace of a Sabbath sky. Begin with hush-light—the opposite of rush hour—a stoplight along the busy highway of time.

THE PRACTICE OF DELIGHT

Sabbath is more than just a fast from the fast lane of life and the world; more than an antidote to our workaholic antics. The Hebrew word for

Time, Twilight, and Eternity

Sabbath comes from the root *Shin-Beit-Tav*, meaning to cease, end, or rest. But *Shabbat* is far from the very opposite of work. While its imposed rest requires not working, that rest isn't idleness. Not just a "day off" and so much more than simple cessation, a true Sabbath is really more about the creative actions of blessing and sanctifying, of hallowing and consecrating. The discipline of keeping a good Sabbath depends on mindfulness, on paying attention to what is most deeply meaningful and true and lasting. "Even when the soul is seared, even when no prayer can come out of our frightened throats," Rabbi Abraham Joshua Heschel wrote, "the clean, silent rest of Sabbath leads to a realm of endless peace, or to the beginning of an awareness of what eternity means."[3]

While the typical work-week increasingly feels something closer to 24/7, it wasn't always and everywhere five days long either. For many of us living and working in the twenty-first century it can be both difficult to remember and intriguing to imagine just how radical the idea of a regular day devoted to rest each week was—and still is. Anciently, rest and leisure were never for those who labored but for those who ruled. Those who oppressed the ancient Jews thought them lazy because of their insistence on observing Sabbath every seventh day. The concept is equally misunderstood today as an archaic, stifling, and restrictive practice of things that must not be done: All abstinence and no fun.

But the Sabbath is more than a day of not-allowed's and not working. Neither is relaxation the point. Rightly understood, the Sabbath isn't even for the purpose of recharging or regaining lost strength in order to have renewed energy to engage in the inevitable work yet to come. "The Sabbath is a day for the sake of life," Rabbi Heschel wrote, "the Sabbath is not for the sake of the weekdays; the weekdays are for the sake of the Sabbath. It is not an interlude but the climax of living."[4]

To the commands to cease and rest are added two others: bless and make holy. In the starshine of Sabbath there is the promise of eternity—of all the time in the world, and more. Sanctify it with all your heart. Indeed, sanctify with all you senses. Take delight, be joyful, and sing praise. Light candles, pray *Kiddush* over a cup of wine, and eat choice foods. Gaze into eternity through faces gathered around the table, through hearts broken open. Recite sacred poetry to each other and make love. The call to observe Sabbath is a call to celebrate the mystery of creation, of us being here.

3. Heschel, *The Sabbath*, 22–23.
4. Ibid., 14.

Together.

And a reminder of just how close eternity is.

That the Sabbath and eternity are of the same essence is a long held belief. The Talmud refers to the Sabbath as somewhat like "the world to come." Rabbi Hayim of Krasne said the Sabbath was the fountainhead of heaven, the spring out from which eternity flows. Rabbi Heschel noted that "the essence of the world to come is Sabbath eternal, and the seventh day in time is an example of eternity."[5] The Sabbath is not just a day, a break in time; it is a foretaste of paradise. Keepers of the Sabbath may not keep the day in eternity, yet eternity is somehow kept in them. The challenge—as it has always been—is how to keep a good Sabbath in a culture that mostly doesn't, a culture that values busyness and equates success with how much we can do, how much we can produce, and consume.

Work and spend.

DWELLING: IN THE MOMENT

Sabbath may be, as Rabbi Heschel so poetically put it, "a palace in time which we build,"[6] but at times it can feel as if that soaring architecture is conjured of nothing but thin air—an idea built on remembrance and intangible hope—and might vanish in the blink of an eye or with one's very next thought. But eternity is more than an endless succession of perishing thoughts or moments. "We hammer wood for a house," the Tao Te Ching says, "but it is the inner space that makes it livable."[7] If we're lucky, we do not pass through time, nor does time pass us by. Rather, time is a realm we inhabit. And when we fully inhabit time—abide in it—we live in eternity. It becomes our home and, if we allow the thought, it is in us as much as we are in it. Our identification with eternity is a curious house, though, one whose construction is never quite finished. Still, the dwelling of our dreams is but a breath away.

Beginning around the third century AD, early Christians seeking a more ascetic way of practicing their faith deliberately sought out the infinite solitude of the desert. The forebears of Christian monasticism, these men (and a few women) became known as the Desert Mothers and Fathers— or more affectionately, Ammas and Abbas—and left a wealth of edifying

---

5. Ibid., 74.
6. Ibid., 15.
7. Lao Tzu, *Tao Te Ching*, 11.

stories and sayings. Despite their humble and meager accommodations, these desert mystics knew a thing or two about building a home in time; many of them abided in prayer, and they all sought to inhabit the scriptures. Any building, they understood, whether built of sturdy stone, wispy palm fronds, ancient words, or focused thoughts, is built in stages and in a certain order. "No one can build a house from the top down; rather you build the foundation first and then build upwards," one desert sage said.[8] Abba Moses asked Abba Silvanus, "Can a man lay a new foundation every day?" The old man replied, "If he works hard he can lay a new foundation at every moment."[9]

Breath by breath we begin again.

We pay attention to whatever task is at hand moment by moment.

Our eternal home is perhaps never quite finished, but even as we pour the foundations of that abode we can also embrace ever new possibilities of what shape it might look like. And our dwellings, from shelter to chateau, have always varied according to our environment and our imagination. "However large, magnificent, and spacious you imagine [the soul] to be, you cannot exaggerate it; the capacity of the soul is beyond all our understanding."[10] So wrote the sixteenth-century Carmelite nun who would later come to be known as Saint Teresa of Ávila. Whereas Rabbi Heschel envisioned the life to come as a palace that we build in time, Saint Teresa saw the soul and its journey to God as an interior castle containing many rooms. In the mystic's crystalline castle, the soul progresses from room to room as it moves from simple to more advanced stages of contemplation and enlightenment. This soul-structure was a second heaven for Teresa in much the same way that the Sabbath was for many Jewish thinkers another form of eternity. And, though *Shabbat* is not specifically a day of prayer only, the approach and entrance to these two buildings is also the same: "As far as I can understand," Teresa wrote, "the gate by which to enter this castle is prayer and meditation."[11]

So, too, are there plenty of distractions to keep us from crossing over that holy threshold between heaven and earth, time and eternity, doing and being—or for that matter, even reaching the castle gate. Even if we somehow manage to find a way to banish all outside interruptions—close the

---

8. Nomura, *Desert Wisdom*, 46.
9. Keller, *Desert Banquet*, 34.
10. Teresa of Ávila, *The Interior Castle*, 11.
11. Ibid., 6.

door of our room to the noises of the world—we are still left alone with the unending noise of our own inner dialogue.

Saint Teresa was not alone in comparing the distracting nature of our thoughts and emotions to feral beasts. The Buddha compared the ceaseless mindless chatter of our minds to a band of drunken monkeys endlessly carrying on and swinging from limb to limb in our brains. Contemporary Buddhists still struggle with taming their "monkey-mind." According to Saint Teresa, a brood of vipers and "venomous reptiles" awaits anyone who dares to venture into even the first of the soul's many rooms, say nothing about the demons that will do anything they can to keep us from the ultimate destination: the treasure of union with God in the castle keep. Our crocodilian thoughts can rise up unbidden and at any time from the murky moat-waters of mindlessness. Miserable mosquitos bred in the standing waters of self-doubt can suck away our attention in a second.

Which is why we build our soul's abode on the firm foundations of faith and tradition, the sure footings of intention and discipline and practice.

IN ETERNITY THERE ARE MANY ROOMS

While a firm foundation is crucial, every one of our foundations rests on common ground: our communal home on earth and in time. Whether it is the practice of delight that is keeping the Sabbath, or the contemplative prayer of the Christian soul, or the mindfulness and attention to thought in meditation, a life built on being is always more lasting than one built on doing. Making a living is one thing; making a being is something else entirely. "One must live to build one's house, and not build one's house to live in."[12] The Sabbath is a joyful example—a holy reminder—of just this kind of doing by being. The same paradoxical action of non-action also animates the Taoist and Zen Buddhist concept of *wu-wei*, which encourages the cultivation of a state of being in which one's actions are effortlessly in alignment with the ebb and flow of the elemental cycles of time and creation. "Practice not-doing," says the Tao Te Ching, "and everything will fall into place."[13]

In Theravada Buddhism monks and lay followers alike honor days known as *Uposatha*. Buddha taught that on these days the mind is cleansed, and the practice includes a more focused reflection and meditation, as well as a ceasing from labor not unlike the Sabbath. For many indigenous

---

12. Bachelard, *The Poetics of Space*, 106.
13. Lao Tzu, *Tao Te Ching*, Mitchell trans., 3.

Time, Twilight, and Eternity

peoples the first day of a new moon is similarly treated. The Cherokee especially consider these lunar moments to be outside the regular perception of time; work is prohibited during what they refer to as the non-days or un-time of the empty moon. Muslims practice *jumu'ah*, or "Friday prayer," in place of Sabbath rest: "When the call is proclaimed to prayer on Friday, hasten earnestly to the Remembrance of Allah, and leave off business" (*The Qur'an*, al-Jumu'ah 62:9).[14]

The Sabbath verbs to cease, rest, bless, and make holy have corresponding counterparts in the Christian Eucharistic liturgy. In the accounts of so many meals in the New Testament, especially those of feasts where loaves and fishes were multiplied (Mark 6:30–44; Luke 9:16), the Last Supper (Matt 26:20; Mark 14:17; Luke 22:14–18; 1 Cor 11:23–26), and Jesus' post-resurrection appearance at Emmaus (Luke 24:13–15), the same four verbs animate the narrative: take, bless, break, and give. Similarly, one could also say that both the Eucharistic liturgy and the holy Sabbath are kindred in their insistence on remembrance over reenactment, albeit in different ways: neither one is a mere portrayal or re-telling of something that once happened sometime in a long ago past.

And, of course, while some keep the Sabbath by going to temple or church, others—like the reclusive Emily Dickinson—keep it staying at home, or in the "cathedral" of the wide open sky, "with a Bobolink for a Chorister—And an Orchard, for a Dome..."[15]

"You must not imagine there are only a few, but a number of rooms," Saint Teresa would have us remember, "For souls enter them by many different ways, and always with good intention."[16] Sabbath is a certain day in time that shapes eternity—that is, if we could all agree on what day that day might be. Or for that matter, even what the measure of a day is. For a brief period of time the French Revolutionists created their own calendar and followed a ten-day week in which each day was ten hours long, each hour composed of one-hundred minutes and each minute made up of one-hundred seconds. To Early Christians, Christ's rising signaled another beginning and so the first day of the week was also for them the eighth. Sabbath is Saturday for some; Sunday for others.

14. Though the next verse, "And when the prayer is ended, disperse within the land and seek from the bounty of Allah..." leads most Muslims not to consider Friday a day of holy rest or Sabbath per se, even if some Muslim countries do consider it a non-work day in the week or count the portion after the Friday prayer as half a rest day.

15. Dickinson, *Collected Poems*, 116.

16. Teresa of Ávila, *The Interior Castle*, 13.

And who's to say there can't be such thing as a Sabbath moment, a Sabbath breath, or even a Sabbath sky?

"We see no need for the setting apart of one day in seven as holy," wrote the great Sioux spokesman Ohíye S'a (also known as Charles Alexander Eastman), "for to us all days belong to God."[17] In fact, eternity might present itself on any day—whether it's the seventh, the first, or the eighth—just as twilight breaks open every day. Who knows? Maybe this is the day. Look out from whatever "room" you happen to be in, and any sunrise and sunset can be a reminder of Creation and blessing if you allow it.

If you hallow it.

IN A WORD, ABIDE

We are not destined to remain the same people we were at various points in our lives—at least, I certainly hope not. "I think one remains the same person throughout," wrote the author of the beloved children's story, *Peter Pan*, "merely passing, as it were, in these lapses of time from one room to another, but all in the same house."[18] The word for "room" Teresa used when she first wrote *The Interior Castle* in her native Spanish was *morada*. It has also been variously translated as "chamber," or "abode." The same can be said of the roomy word in the line from the Johanine gospel that surely must have informed Teresa's vision: "In my Father's house there are many rooms" (John 14:2). The word most often translated as "room" in that rather well-known passage is the Greek word *monai*. But depending on which translation one settles on, heaven can also have many dwelling places—or even *mansions*, a word whose definition easily resonates with Teresa's vision of a crystalline soul-castle or Rabbi Heschel's palace in time.

In Italian a room is a *stanza*, a word that can also mean an arrangement of written lines and from which some of the world's most beautiful poems have been built, and then dreamily inhabited by so many readers. In fact, words are quite often not unlike little castles unto themselves, each with their chambers and interconnected hallways, their turrets and towers. Step over any one of their thresholds—providing its drawbridge is down—and they can reveal to the adventurous of mind as many rooms and as complex an architecture as their most magnificent medieval counterparts.

---

17. In Nerburn, *The Soul of an Indian*, 15.
18. Barrie, *Peter Pan*, 396.

Time, Twilight, and Eternity

If this all seems like more than a little word play and poetic license, it isn't. Ask any adherent of any faith tradition and they'll tell you the words of their holiest scriptures are not simply markings on a page or scroll but living, breathing texts. The Sabbath, the Interior Castle—or any of the eternal abodes we build in time—are all poems we literally inhabit room by room and compose stanza by stanza. And just as the threshold is to space and twilight is to time, the practices of attention, mindfulness, and prayer allow us to cross over into those immortal lines.

We build our spacious poem in time not by the strength of our hands, the sweat of our brow, or with carpenter's tools. We construct our interior castle by some mysterious force, as if by instinct, like the inspiration of our lungs or the way a particular word or image can inspire us to daydreaming. Or the way a bird builds its home. The materials for a nest may be gathered by beak and talon, but the instrument that ultimately prescribes the form for the interior of the nest, where the bird resides, is nothing else but the body of the bird itself turning round and round in time and space. Therefore, as the French naturalist Jules Michelet concluded, the bird and its nest are inseparable and can be thought of as one in the same:

> The result is obtained only by a constantly repeated pressure of the breast: there is not one blade of grass that, in order to catch and keep the curve, has not been pressed on countless times by the bird's breast, its heart. . . . The house is the same as the person.[19]

When questioned about the world to come, Jesus responded "The kingdom of God is within you" (Luke 17:21 KJV). "Like living stones, let yourselves be built into a spiritual house" wrote the author of the First Epistle of Peter (1 Pet 2:5). We build our soul's abode in the same manner as the heart-shaped nest. As the swallow and the phoebe gather bits and pieces of the world around them, so do we shape eternity into our home by gathering moments and pressing them to our human breast. It is just as precarious a thing as any bird's dwelling. Yet, like any nest, it sets us to daydreaming of safety and home and belonging.

And something eternal in us is incubated there.

Just as Plato insisted that we become what we behold, so too do we become, in a very real way, the space we inhabit. And no matter how far we stray from inhabiting time—from keeping a Sabbath practice and abiding in eternity—there is always an invitation to begin again. It is only ever in the human dimension of time that we can realize resurrection, the generative

---

19. Cited in Bachelard, *Poetics of Space*, 100–01.

and regenerative nature of every instant, and that every moment is an act of creation and therefore holy. Not just each day, but each moment offers us the chance to lay a new foundation that can support and uphold our daily work in time and space.

Thank God.

Because when it comes to practicing Sabbath—well, I, for one, need a lot of practice.

But then again, perhaps we'll never get it quite right.

(That is, until we do.)

BEGIN AGAIN

But we do not begin all over again at point zero. Neither are we destined to repeat over and over the most primary lesson: that one and one simply make two. Rather, we circle back to what we already know knowing a little bit more and add to the total sum, always returning and expanding exponentially like a snail builds its shell around the axis of a perfect spiral, a slow but steady process of formation. If one and one make two; two plus one make three, and three plus two equals five. In mathematics this pattern is known as the Fibonacci sequence, where each number comes from adding the two numbers before it:

1, 1, 2, 3, 5, 8, 13, 21, 34, 55, 89, 144, and so on.

Named after a thirteenth-century Italian mathematician, the sequence has even more ancient and poetic roots in measuring meter in Sanskrit prose, the number of syllables in a unit of verse. In nature it can mathematically explain not only the elegant spiral of the snail's shell but also the spinning center of a sunflower, the fiddlehead of the fern frond when it first emerges from the earth, the grapevine's winding tendril, whirling galaxies (including our own), and the coiling cochlea bone inside our heads that thinks it hears the whisper of waves from some far-off ocean when we hold a spiraling seashell up to our wondering ear.

Perhaps the rooms of time we are meant to create from within and inhabit are most elegantly revealed in the transcendent geometry of the spiraling shell. Those ever-enlarging compartments successively dwelt in by sea- and land-creatures alike inspired the nineteenth-century poet Oliver Wendell Holmes to write what would become one of his most famous poems, *The Chambered Nautilus*, of whose concluding lines Saint Teresa would surely approve:

> Build thee more stately mansions, O my soul,
> As the swift seasons roll!
> Leave thy low-vaulted past!
> Let each new temple, nobler than the last,
> Shut thee from heaven with a dome more vast,
> Till thou at length art free,
> Leaving thine outgrown shell by life's unresting sea![20]

From ancient ages to modern times the spiraling shell has fascinated the careful observer as an object of particular significance worthy of reflection and contemplation. Fossilized remains of prehistoric ammonites reveal a spiraling force at least as old as the Mesozoic Age. The tombs of our earliest ancestors were often strewn with shells, a funerary custom we can only wonder at and guess its significance. For the Ancients the shell, both its hard covering and its sentient organism, embodied not only form and formation, but was also the symbol of the human being in its entirety: body and soul. Just as the human body encloses the soul in an outside envelope, and the soul quickens the entire being, so too did the shell enclose the essential organism of the mollusk. Thus, it was believed, the human body became as lifeless as an empty shell when the soul took its leave. It seems we've long sensed something of the eternal in the sheltering spiral of the shell, wondered about beginnings and endings and circling back to things in its ever-returning form.

The planet spins, tilted on its axis just so, and creation continues to unfold.

Always we begin again.

We bend down and pick up a shell at our feet; hold a spiral of time to our ear, and wonder. If we're lucky, someone next to us holds the shell of time up to our ear and says tenderly, "listen, you can hear eternity." "Abide in me, as I abide in you," Jesus is reported to have said (John 15:4). And perhaps, that is how eternity truly breaks open in time, and what we are all meant to do: abide in each other; bring a Sabbath consciousness to our every relationship so that others may find peace and rest and refuge in us. To become living Sabbath-shells to one another, echoing the immortal, primordial, unresting sea from which we all emerge.

To become palaces and castles and temples of time that walk the earth.

Till *all* at length art free.

---

20. Holmes, *The Autocrat of the Breakfast-table*, 111.

Burning the Midnight Oil

There are perhaps few other images that so invoke reverie than the flickering bit of light from the wick of a candle or lamp—at least, so it seems from the brightly illuminated perspective of modern life after electricity. For our earliest ancestors the flame was no mere metaphor; nightfall meant huddling together around a carefully tended watch fire. Today when daylight begins to fade and darkness begins to gather we simply flick a switch and a full spectrum of light quite un-miraculously fills whatever space we happen to be in. (We don't even need a switch if we are too troubled to flick it; these days automatic timers, fully-networked home systems and remote controls accessed via computerized tablets and smart-phones digitally and diligently keep us out of the dark.) Ubiquitous light even floods outdoor fields and stadiums so we can go out and play all hours of the night, a thought that never would have even crossed the minds of our fire-lit forebears. Indeed, before the lightbulb ever went off above Edison's head, twilight must have been an anxious time. Fast fell the eventide.

Were the candles set and the flint at hand?

Were the lamps filled with oil and their wicks trimmed?

Even Edison, who dreamed in the not-so-very-long-ago about the possibility of more easily illuminating the dark, would be down-right gob smacked at the developments in lighting since the "simple" electric lightbulb of his invention. Far more efficient light-emitting diodes (LEDs) and spirals of compact fluorescence now illuminate our homes and workplaces and parking lots. More than ever before, the lamp and candle are anachronisms: quite literally flickering lights that have been all but put out. Who could imagine today lighting up to twenty-thousand candles so that the flames could be reflected off an equally ridiculous number of mirrors and

Time, Twilight, and Eternity

crystal chandeliers to illuminate the great hall of the palace at Versailles (even if you were a Sun King, like Louis XIV), or how voraciously ancient temples and medieval cathedrals consumed candles, especially on Sabbaths and feast days? Yet we still place the illuminating fires of the candle and the lamp on our altars and shrines—or at the very least, our mantels and dining tables—not so much as source of light but symbol of something else: the *idea* of a light in the darkness, or perhaps even the light of divinity itself.

The French philosopher Bachelard wrote an entire meditation on the metaphoric properties of firelight and its pull on the human psyche and imagination, in which he mused:

> Long ago, in a long ago even dreams themselves have forgotten, the flame of a candle made wise men think; it provided the solitary philosopher with a thousand dreams. On his table, next to objects imprisoned in their shapes, next to those books that teach one so slowly, the flame of the candle summoned endless thoughts and aroused immeasurable images . . . . Is not the world alive in a flame?[1]

The ceremonial or ritual use of firelight has long been a part of the practice of faith. The ancient Greeks and Romans each had their own sacred fires and tended to votive lamps kept eternally aflame before statues of their deities. Lamps have long been lit daily (most often at dusk, but also at dawn) and placed before the altar in Hindu homes—and Sikhs, Jains, and Hindus all light festive lamps on Diwali, a celebration of good over evil, knowledge over ignorance, and inner light over spiritual darkness. Similarly, candles and lamps and incense are placed before shrines to, or images of the Buddha in honor of the illumination given by the Awakened One's teachings. In a chapter fittingly titled *al-Nur*, or "The Light," Islam's Holy Qur'an compares the illuminative nature of Allah to that of a celestial lamp:

> Allah is the Light of the heavens and the earth. The example of His light is like a niche within which is a lamp, the lamp is within glass, the glass as if it were a pearly white star lit from the oil of a blessed olive tree, neither of the east nor of the west, whose oil would almost glow even if untouched by fire. Light upon light. . . . (Sūrah al-Nur 24:35)

The lamp, the oil, candles, and their respective lights, were all crucial elements in the life of the ancient Israelites, both in the household and in

---

1. Bachelard, *The Flame of a Candle*, 13.

the temple. The Hebrew Scriptures reveal that as far back as the Book of Exodus the lighting of the lamp was an integral component of worship for the faithful, where Aaron is commanded to burn fragrant incense at the altar as he tends to the temple lamps each morning and evening, "so incense will burn regularly before the Lord for generations to come" (Exod 30:7–8). The prescribed instruction and ritual of creating, placing, and tending to the night lantern shimmers throughout the book of Leviticus as well (e.g., 24:1–4), and lights the way all through the Psalms, as in: "Your word is a lamp for my feet, a light on my path" (Ps 119:105).[2] And the Talmud teaches that just as a lamp is called a lamp, so too might we call the soul of man a lamp.

In addition to the lighting of the Shabbat candles on Friday evening to signal the beginning of the weekly Sabbath celebration in Judaism, there is another ritual candle composed of multiple wicks braided together which is lit on the following evening to mark the conclusion of the Sabbath and the beginning of the new week.[3] The candles in every Hanukkah menorah pay tribute not only to the rededication of the temple in Jerusalem but also to the miracle when, at that rededication the small amount of ritual oil in the lamps—barely enough for one day—lasted for a full eight days. Even after the destruction of the temple in Jerusalem, the Jews did not forget the rite of kindling the evening light; whenever and wherever they performed this ritual act of devotion they were offering praise and glory to the One who, in the lovely words of their *Ma'ariv*, or evening prayer, "creates day and night, rolling away the light before the darkness and darkness before the light," the One "who evenings the evening."

And evenings the evening still.

---

2. The most lamp-lit book of the Hebrew Bible is by far Exodus: in addition to the passages cited, prescriptions regarding the temple lamp appear in Exodus 25:31–39; 27:20–21; and 37:17–24. The lamp also makes an appearance in: Numbers (8:1–4); 2 Samuel (21:17; 22:29); 1 Kings (15:4); 1 Chronicles (28:15); 2 Chronicles (4:7, 20–21; and 13:11); and Proverbs (6:23; 132:17; and 20:27).

3. The ceremony known as Havdalah, meaning separation or division, and which marks the moment in between the Sabbath and the week to come is yet another twilight prayer time. The ritual begins just after sunset, when three stars are visible in the night sky, and involves welcoming the work week by lighting the special Havdalah candle, blessing a cup of wine, and inhaling the fragrance of sweet spices (either branches of aromatic herbs or a special container of cloves kept just for this purpose). Havdalah ends with a blessing marking the division between sacred and secular time—between being and doing, the end of holy rest and the beginning of the work of co-creation—and with its observers blessing each other for the coming week.

All of this is to say that both the candle and the lamp have always been as much about kilowatts and candle-power per square foot and physically lighting a dark space as they have been about the poetry of illumination and the proclamation of the ineffable, the incendiary, and the incandescent.

So too can tradition and truth be passed like a flame from one candle to another.

ENDURING LIGHT

The pattern of the ancient hymn of creation that opens the Hebrew Scriptures—"and there was evening, and there was morning—the first day" (Gen 1:5)—is reflected in religious practice and observance around the globe and to this very day. The twin turning points of dusk and dawn continue to be important and auspicious times of prayer across faith traditions. Like so many Jewish religious before them, the earliest Christians also measured their days from sunset to sunset and began their daily prayers with the approaching dark, when anciently the night lanterns were lighted. While the secular clock begins and ends the day these days otherwise, the Christian liturgical day still begins in the gloaming with the sanctification of evening and with a service of prayer deeply rooted in *Ma'ariv*—the ancient Hebrew tradition of lamp-lighting and evening prayer—the office which early Christians called the *Lucernarium*, or the "Service of Light."

Jesus himself would have participated in the ancient rite of kindling light; he had grown up in the Hebrew tradition, after all, as had the first disciples to follow him. The first Christians retained much of that sacred tradition, especially when it came to daily prayer: "Every day they continued to meet together in the temple courts," we read in the Acts of the Apostles (2:46). And in another chapter of that New Testament book: "one day Peter and John were going up to the temple at the time of prayer" (Acts 3:1). It has been said that, for Christians, baptism replaced the Jewish rite of circumcision, and the sacrifice embodied in the Eucharist replaced the sacrificial offerings of the Old Testament. But nothing replaced the rite of gathering together and lighting the night lantern, taking care to light each other's lamps to carry back home, thus linking together the movements of the secular day with the spiritual life, natural light with supernatural illumination, and the temporal with the eternal.

In the New Testament, Jesus is twice recorded as saying the human eye is "the lamp of the body" (Matt 6:22; Luke 11:34), and can illuminate our entire being: "Therefore, if your whole body is full of light, and no part of it dark, it will be just as full of light as when a lamp shines its light on you" (Luke 11:36). This is what really seemed to catch fire for the early Christians; this re-imagined, re-apportioned, and re-embodied interpretation of lamplight. For them the lamp brought to remembrance the one who not only called himself "the light of the world" (John 8:12), but taught that they also were that saving light—as are we today (Matt 5:14). The lighting of the night lantern at every gathering for prayer invoked and recalled the spiritual presence among them of their teacher. The New Testament concludes with the image of "a new heaven and a new earth" where there is need for neither the sun nor the moon and in which the glory of God is the only light and Christ is the lamp (Rev 21:1–27).

ETERNAL FLAME

In this more secular age it seems fewer and fewer people gather for worship or prayer even once a week. But early on it was quite normal for church communities to gather at dusk and at dawn every day. As early as the second century the Roman governor Pliny the Younger complained about the curious behavior of the "bothersome" early Christians, including morning and evening gatherings where they sang songs to Christ as if he were a god. Writing not long after that, Tertullian, considered by many the father of western theology, tenderly described one such gathering in the gloaming: "After manual ablution and the bringing in of lights, each person is asked to stand forth and sing, as he can, a hymn to God, either one from the Holy Scriptures or one from his own heart."[4] Cyprian, the third-century martyred bishop of Carthage, wrote of evening prayer:

> . . . at the sunsetting and the decline of the day, of necessity we must pray again. For since Christ is the true sun and the true day, as the worldly sun and worldly day depart, when we pray and ask that light may return to us again, we pray for the advent of Christ, which shall give us the grace of everlasting light.[5]

One of the first documentations of a particular Christian liturgy or doxology surrounding the lighting or bringing in of the lamp appears in the writings of Hippolytus of Rome (c. 215, CE) which relate that a deacon

---

4. In Roberts Donaldson, *The Ante-Nicene Fathers*, 47.
5. In Uspensky, *Evening Worship in the Orthodox Church*, 105.

carried in the lamp and stood among those gathered and recited, among other prayers, a thanksgiving for illumination in the dark.[6] By the fourth century the words of "O Gladsome Light," a vesperal hymn sung at the earliest *Lucernaria* and still at the core of Christian evening prayer today, were already considered age-old tradition by Saint Basil the Great, who wrote of this hymn: "We cannot say who composed these words of thanksgiving at the lighting of the lamps, but the people use these ancient words."[7] In fact, the *Phos Hilaron*, as the hymn is known in its original New Testament Greek is, indeed, ancient. The words sung at the setting of the sun by the faithful both then and now—"As fades the day's last light we see the lamps of night, / Our common hymn outpouring, / O God of might unknown"[8]— shine with a relic light and compose the earliest known Christian hymn outside of those recorded in the Bible.

One fourth-century pilgrim to the Holy Land, recorded in her diary an account of an evening prayer as she observed it at the Church of the Resurrection in Jerusalem: "A flame is not brought in from outside," she noted, "but is obtained within the holy sepulcher, where day and night a lamp constantly burned."[9] As the flame was brought in and used to ignite the lamps and candles throughout, the congregation sang vesperal psalms and other more lengthy antiphons, by the end of which "it was dusk."[10] While Egeria referred to this liturgy as others had before her—The Service of Light—the tradition as it was carried out in the earliest monasteries (perhaps even more faithfully) was by then also called *Vespertina solemnitas*, a name in which we can recognize the twilight prayer and service that is now more simply known and practiced amongst Christians as "Vespers."

O GLADSOME LIGHT

Whether whispering to themselves in their cells or gathered together in community, what the early Christian monks understood was that neither a lamp nor an ordained leader is required in any service to the light. They

---

6. In Dix, *The Apostolic Tradition of Hippolytus of Rome*, 51.

7. Basil of Caesarea, *St. Basil the Great, on the Holy Spirit*, 110.

8. The poet Robert S. Bridges' translation, which first appeared in the *Yattendon Hymnal* (1899). See also Polman, Stulken, and Sydnor, *Amazing Grace: Hymn Texts for Devotional Use*, 283.

9. Wilkinson, *Egeria's Travels*, 3.

10. Ibid., 124.

were simply monks, after all, not priests, and in addition likely lacked the resources necessary to procure the oil, wax, and flint required for lamp-lighting. Yet they maintained a rich and deep prayer life. In fact, the prayer service of Vespers (as opposed to Eucharistic services) has always been a more egalitarian affair, presided over not by any member of the clergy but by common lay folk. Even in what is perhaps the most elaborate and "High-Church" incarnation of Vespers—Evensong, or the choral setting of evening prayer in the Anglican and Episcopal Church—it is still about the communion of human voices in praise of Creation, an act of community and the expression of all those assembled. And in that same tradition, lay people continue to gather in their own homes as the sun sets below the horizon, and turn to the section of *The Book of Common Prayer* entitled: "Daily Devotions for Individuals and Families" in service to their private and/or familial practice of evening prayer.[11]

Emerson wrote that we should strive to become the day itself. Rilke was more specific: we should become our evening prayer, he thought, "become Evensong."[12] In the Christian tradition alone there are differing perspectives of what prayer can look like. The light of Vespers itself varies according to whether it shines out from the Catholic, Protestant, or Eastern Orthodox traditions. Yet any prayer or set of words with which we seek the Divine Mystery is never the same thing as the tender act of prayer itself, regardless of what tradition we may practice or honor. Neither should prayer be restricted solely to the realm of religion, or for that matter even spirituality. Both the astronomer's outer universe as seen through the lens of a telescope and the monk's inner universe glimpsed by the mind's eye can equally provoke astonishment and reverence—and rightfully so.

There are so many wonderful prayers from so many traditions. And there is also the irrevocably unique and intimate prayer that can only come from each one of us in all of space and time: a candle in the wind, one whose flame lives on long after it is ever kindled and shone into the dark. The same flame, according to Hindu scripture, flickers in the sun as in the earth as well as in our hearts (Maitre Upanishad 6:17). "The day will come," predicted the Jesuit philosopher Teilhard de Chardin, "when, after harnessing the ether, the winds, the tides, gravitation, we shall harness for God the energies of love. And on that day, for the second time in the history

---

11. See *The Book of Common Prayer*, 139–140, an invaluable resource for those wishing to explore such daily practice.

12. See his poem cycle "The Book of Pilgrimage" in *Rilke's Book of Hours*, 135.

Time, Twilight, and Eternity

of the world, man will have discovered fire."[13] Every day the sun lingers at the horizon; shadows lengthen and darkness gathers. And as the eventide falls so do we. We bend our human bodies into one of the innumerable shapes of prayer: we fall to our knees, or sit cross-legged, or we stand and raise our hands to our hearts or to the sky; we light a candle or lamp, or we whisper into the dark; we lift our voices, or bow down and kiss the ground; we whirl around, or press our palms together, or fold our fingers into any number of age-old gestures. There is nothing quite like the human body at prayer—naming, thanking, beseeching, proclaiming, remembering, praising, longing, belonging—entering into the primal rhythm of life itself as the planet slowly, surely spins silently through space.

---

13. Teilhard de Chardin, *Toward the Future*, 86–87.

ENTR'ACTE

Night

Dark Matters

"A great cause of the night is lack of the sun,"[1] Shakespeare wryly observed—although it isn't necessarily the cause that has long concerned us night after night, but the effect: pitch-black darkness (and whatever lurks within its inky shadows). Night is one thing, but darkness is quite another. It isn't difficult to associate the dwindling of daylight with the end of promise, the dying of the brightness with the inevitability of all endings. But really, the unavoidable dark is our primordial home; not where we end, but where we begin. In the beginning, even before "before," there was only darkness and everything was in it, although the earth as we know it was not yet formed.

And then there was light . . .

"God saw that the light was good, and God separated the light from the darkness. God called the light 'day' and the darkness 'night.' And there was evening, and there was morning—the first day" (Gen 1:1–5). Or put another way: more than thirteen-billion years ago there was a singular cosmic event that unleashed time and space and everything we can ever know or imagine. Either way, darkness and nothingness preceded the light—and always have. Before there was ever evening or morning, before any first day ever dawned, there was a day without any yesterday when only "darkness covered the surface of the deep" (Gen 1:2). Light did not come out of some preexistent light, but out of a primordial darkness. Still, we do not equate the still of the night with life and creation, or even the hope of a new day. Rather, night is the place where we lose our way; where "geography comes to an end," as Merton wrote, and our "Compass has lost all earthly north."[2]

We are not nocturnal creatures.

---

1. Shakespeare, *As You Like It*, III.ii.25., in *The Complete Works*, 791.
2. Merton, "Sacred Heart 2 (A Fragment—)" in *Collected Poems*, 24.

Time, Twilight, and Eternity

Every child of the light knows that the night makes us vulnerable; the dark is where wolves howl and teeth gnash. If we do not bury our heads under the blankets and try to sleep through it, we attempt to banish the dark with artificial light of one kind or another. Things go bump in the night. That's why we call the darkness the witching hour, the hour of the wolf, the still of the night . . . the dead of night. We only make up words for things that matter, after all, experiences that we feel a need to talk about or contain. We crave care-free and bright sunshiny days, not some dark night of the soul. We do not seek endarkenment, but enlightenment and illumination. To be "in the dark" about something is the opposite: to be lost, clueless, unaware, a dithering dolt.

The dark night—whether of the senses or the soul—is an age-old trial. Not only is it an ancient phenomenon, the dark night also knows no religious bounds. In every faith tradition, mystics and saints and prophets have written eloquently of the dark night, of perceived abandonment, or of longing and desire for communion with the divine. "As the deer pants for streams of water, so my soul pants for you, my God" the Hebrew Bible tenderly laments (Ps 42:1). An entire surah, or chapter, of the Qur'an underscores the importance of such longing. Entitled *Al-Layl*, or "The Night," it begins: "By the night as it envelops," and ends: "Those who constantly cherish only intense longing to encounter the essential face of their Lord will attain complete realization" (*The Qur'an*, al-Layl 92:1, 20–21.)

The dark night abided in the fifth mansion of Teresa of Ávila's interior castle of a life built of prayer. For the Italian poet Dante Alighieri, the dark night was "a dark wood"—the entryway into the first of three rings of human consciousness: "Inferno," or Hell—while others have called the dark night dazzling, or likened it to a cloud of unknowing or even a ray of divine shadow. The Christian mystic Saint John of the Cross famously found the light of his heart in the dark night of his soul—and then graciously called the night a "luminous darkness."

And yet, no matter how hard I pray each evening, ". . . even the darkness will not be dark to you. . ." (Ps 139:12), the night never shines as bright as the day. The dark is as dark and as inevitable and familiar as it is unwelcome. There is a sure and dependable darkness that descends daily and at every setting of the sun. And there is the darkness we experience some times in life of sadness, disappointment, or even loss. Sometimes that's all it is: a difficult time in life to be endured. But then there is another darkness that can also descend: the darkness of the soul or spirit which we tend

DARK MATTERS

to ignore, deny, dismiss or attempt to avoid at all costs—a dark night that tests our faith. Even though we know it's useless, we count the midnight hours and minutes—both the optically dark hours that gather each day at dusk, as well as the psychological and spiritual darkness that stalks within them—because we know how slippery doubt can be in the dark, how easily it can slither into something much more sinister.

"Within light there is darkness," advises one eighth-century Buddhist teaching, "but do not try to understand that darkness—within darkness there is light, but do not look for that light [for] light and darkness are a pair, like the foot before and the foot behind, in walking."[3] Placing one foot in front of the other is one thing during the day, especially for us humans; we walk upright in the sunshine. But our greatest obstacle has always been how not to stumble in the night. Try as we might, we can never banish the dark altogether; even when we light a lamp or candle, that flame brings all manner of shadows to life. We ourselves cast a shadow into the world regardless of where we stand. Perhaps all we can ever hope for is to learn how to walk in the dark. Or as Saint Paul suggested, how to walk not just by sight, but also by faith (2 Cor 5:7).

The Hebrew Scriptures tell us that God said the light was good and called it "day," but what if we put words into God's mouth because we were simply afraid of the dark and what the night might bring?

What if in the beginning was not daybreak . . . but heartbreak?

Loneliness and fear?

Begin here, with what many scholars of the Bible propose: that the opening lines of the Book of Genesis are not the oldest Judeo-Christian scripture we have—that, in fact, none of the Pentateuch (the first five books of the Old Testament) is the oldest book of the Bible, but that the anonymously written Book of Job was the first to be written down. That the beginning was neither the word nor the light; not *logos*, but something closer to *pathos*, to experience and suffering: the story of one man, an ancient ancestor, wrestling with the misery of everyday existence. Yet, every Bible begins with that primordial phrase from Genesis: "In the beginning." Poor ol' Job doesn't usually show up until some nineteen books later basically asking the same question we still ask today: Where is God in human suffering?[4]

---

3. A teaching of the master Shitou Xiqian, cited in Strand, *Waking Up to the Dark*, 138.

4. Concerning the date and authorship of the Book of Job see, for example, Kugler and

Time, Twilight, and Eternity

"I cry out to you, God, but you do not answer" (Job 30:20a).

We fear the dark and worship the light, and always have at least since our Neolithic forebears somehow managed to arrange those huge hunks of rock at Stonehenge into a perfect solar calendar and temple to light and shadow, if not before. The dark was where evil lurked. We know better now—not that there is no evil in the dark, but that it can show up at any hour anywhere around the globe. We've always stood—and stand still—before the dark night wondering, fearing, and doubting. Even today we open the door and find, as did Edgar Allen Poe, perhaps the greatest poet of the raven-dark night, so long ago: "Darkness there, and nothing more."[5]

Yet it is not merely nothing that we peer into. There *is* something more—a lot more.

We are not much changed since the ancients, who all worshipped the light. The Egyptians had their sun god Ra; the Greeks sang hymns to Helios; and the Aztec and Mayans mapped out time according to their solar deities. Among the Vedic Sanskrit hymns still recited by many Hindus is the *gāyatrī mantra*—dedicated to the sun deity Savitr. Devout Jews who wear the Tallit, or prayer shawl, still praise Adonai, saying "arrayed in glory and majesty, You wrap Yourself with light as with a garment. . ." as they wrap themselves in the prayer-soaked fringes of their shawl.[6] The psalmist wrote we should rejoice in the *day* the Lord has made, not in the night (Ps 118:24).[7]

"God is light," wrote Saint John in the New Testament, "and in him there is no darkness at all" (1 John 1:5). In Matthew's gospel Jesus insists we are that light. Muslims address Allah as an exquisite, encouraging, and guiding flame; Buddhists follow the teachings of the "Enlightened One." We all equate darkness with sin or ignorance, and sometimes even evil—or at least the opposite of anything holy. Instead of saying, "I'll pray for you," some folks say, "I will hold you in the light." It seems no matter where we ground our faith we're all inevitably drawn to the light, like determined moths to an immolating flame. None other than Albert Einstein, himself,

---

Hartin, *An Introduction to the Bible*; and Seow, *Job 1–21: Interpretation and Commentary*.

5. A line from his poem "The Raven," in *Great Tales and Poems*, 302.

6. See "Order of Putting on the Tallith" in *Prayer Book for the New Year*, 20; *Gates of Prayer*, 48.

7. While the Hebrew word *"yom"* can be used to mean time in general, or even the time from one sunset to another sunset—as in twenty-four hours—it is generally translated to mean a day in terms of sunrise to sunset—that is to say, a period of light, e.g., the translation in the Orthodox Jewish Bible (OJB): "This is the *yom* which *Hashem* hath made; let us rejoice and be glad in it" (Ps 118:24).

said that he spent his whole life trying to understand the true nature of light.

And yet, God seems to abide not in light, but it's opposite: darkness. The divine always seems to be rising up out of the dark night. Solomon said God dwells in a cloud of darkness (1Kgs 8:12). Similarly, in the saga of the ancient Israelites' long journey from slavery in Egypt through the wilderness and to the "Promised Land," the prophet Moses received their holy covenant by approaching "the thick darkness where God was" (Exod 20:21). Indeed, darkness is God's cloak, the psalmist sang (Ps 18:11). It was night—"the lamp of God had not yet gone out"—when God decided to call to young Samuel and make him a prophet (1 Sam 3). In fact, throughout the ages, those who have heard the voice of God almost always heard it whispering to them in the middle of the night; the holy revealing itself to those who wait or walk in the dark. Muhammad's mystic travel to the seven heavens, where he received divine instruction on the details of prayer to take back to the faithful, was not a day-lit journey: "Glory to (Allah) Who did take His servant for a Journey *by night* from the Sacred Mosque to the farthest. . ." (*The Qur'an*, al-Isrā' 17:1, emphasis added).

Ultimately, any dark night provokes the same questions about boundaries and limits, about beginnings and endings. Where does light begin, we wonder, and where does darkness end? What are the boundaries of outer space? Of inner darkness? Is darkness simply, as Aristotle, and others would have it, the passive absence of light—or is it a more active presence itself, as Goethe suggested (and we know deep down in our hearts)? For that matter, how does one even begin to measure absence? Or would we even want to? Why is the night sky even dark? Why isn't it, with its billions of nocturnal suns burning in space, as brightly lit as the most glorious sapphire sky of a summer day? Why have we always linked the dark with evil, with grief, with sadness? And how is it that we describe that sadness with the same color as we do the supernal happy-go-lucky blue skies lit by our sun? Darkness and light—melancholy and joyfulness—are not the same; they're as different as . . . well, as night and day.

Inevitably, our longing for divine light invokes the opposite: a soul-searing encounter with spiritual darkness. We are correct in thinking there is a hidden power in the dark night; we've only—whether knowingly or unknowingly—misinterpreted that power. And so we pray:

Vouchsafe, O Lord, to keep us this night. . .

Let Your mercy be upon us. . .

Preserve us from our ghostly foe...
We pray: "Grant us a quiet night and a perfect end."

NIGHT SHIFT

For many, the dark has long been the only place where, paradoxically, there is any chance of finding illumination. The psychiatrist Carl Jung cautioned against denying our darker thoughts and emotions and living only as children of light. In every faith tradition there have been those who woke in the middle of the night to pray or chant or meditate. Faithful Jews practice *Tikkun Chatzot*, or the "Midnight Repair," after a line from the Psalms that says, "At midnight I rise to give you thanks" (Ps 119:62). *Tahajjud* is the night prayer for Muslims. Similarly, in the Christian Liturgy of the Hours, *Matins*, or *Vigils*, is prayed during the night or at midnight. We ought to seek for answers in the darkness, not daylight, counseled the Franciscan theologian Bonaventure. According to the poet Rilke, the flame of any candle "limits the world to the circle it illumines," whereas "the dark embraces everything . . ."[8] When confronted with loss or doubt, or any "tearing problem," Walt Whitman's suggestion was to seek out "the last voiceless satisfaction" of the starry night sky: "In silence of a fine night," he wrote, "such questions are answered to the soul, the best answers that can be given."[9]

The stars aren't the only things in the night sky, though; there's all that blackness in which they burn. Look up at the sky on a clear night and you can clearly see there is a whole lot more of that (whatever it is) than light in the universe. In fact, most of the cosmos is what astronomers call dark matter, detectable only by the gravitational pull it exerts; as little as five percent of the universe is composed of stuff we can actually observe directly. The remaining ninety-five percent remains hidden in the shadows: dark matter, dark energy, or whatever it is that continues to cause our universe to exist; to hold together, expand, and accelerate. There's a whole lot more to the dark than we can see. For every wonder we can observe and explain there are countless speechless others we do not—perhaps even cannot—see or know.

Imagine a point in another galaxy in the universe. Now try to imagine, due to the natural expansion of the universe, that same point will be millions of miles further away tonight than it was last night. Astonishing! Right? We

---

8. See his poem cycle "The Book of Monastic Life," in *Rilke's Book of Hours*, 63.
9. In Werness, "Whitman and van Gogh," 35–41.

might as well try to count how many angels can dance on the head of a pin. And yet, the universe has always turned out to be full of surprises and more mind-boggling than any religious or scientist could ever dream. Eventually (as in a millennium or trillenium, or longer) all of the stars overhead will have become so distant that their light will be imperceptible to our human eyes. Then, if there are any of us left here to look up at the night sky generations hence, we will raise our eyes and see... "Darkness there, and nothing more." Only emptiness and void, not unlike the cosmic beginnings of our beginning-less beginning—and the poet Eliot will have predicted correctly that in our end is indeed our beginning.[10]

Creation continues.

Something out of nothing.

Everything that was, is, and will be is still becoming and expanding—and gaining velocity . . . an infinite, phosphorescent having-been that is somehow still beginning, still unfolding.

Begin before any flame ever flickered, then, or any star spangled.

Begin before the earth revolved around the sun; with just us thinking we were the center of the universe, the shining light above our heads revolving around us during the day and, inexplicably, extinguishing itself with every black night. Begin before Copernicus, before Galileo, before Hubble and Kepler and Tycho Brahe. Begin before we ever imagined mountains on the moon, or other moons circling other planets, or us walking on the moon. Begin before eclipse and comet could ever be explained or predicted. Begin before rings ever circled Saturn; before Jupiter or Neptune. Begin with one planet—ours—or with nine, or more, or less; begin before we ever considered or reconsidered Pluto; before gravity or ellipsis or orbit. Begin with one solar system—ours—before we knew there were billions more; begin before Andromeda or the Milky Way, before nuclei or nebulae or supernovae, and with a finite universe.

Begin before light years or black holes; before quarks or quantum theory. Before the distinct possibility that even the universe is not singular.

Begin with the stars in our eyes.

Our universe has always been expanding. We may be used to the idea of outer space today, but it wasn't always so. At first we believed the firmament was a solid dome that stretched like a celestial roof above our heads. The stars and the sun and the moon were all fixed within that same plane,

---

10. See "Little Gidding," from his poem cycle "The Four Quartets" in *Collected Poems*, 208.

and it was so near birds could fly to its farthest edge. Now we have no idea where that edge might be; no matter how close we think we get, it always seems to have moved on ahead of us—which it has (and is)... at the speed of light.

In the early seventeenth century Galileo, looking through one of the first predecessors of what would become the telescope, saw that there were far more stars in the universe than anyone up to then had ever imagined. In 1610 his "spyglass" revealed that Jupiter did not spin all alone, but was accompanied by multiple moons. Less than half a century later astronomers were crafting elegant and compound telescopes designed to look ever deeper into space. Isaac Newton added a reflector; Chester Moore Hall, an achromatic lens. Others found a way to increase the size of the reflector without distorting the image, or to refine the process of silvering glass mirrors. Although our thinking by then had expanded exponentially, we still thought the Milky Way Galaxy was the whole of the universe.

Larger and ever more powerful telescopes were built, and by the middle of the nineteenth century William Parsons had constructed what was then the largest reflector telescope, known as the "Leviathan of Parsonstown." Physics and gravity tested the limits of the ever-growing lenses and mirrors—two meters, five meters, ten meters—as we tried to keep up with the expanding universe. It wasn't until 1924, when Edwin Hubble scientifically confirmed the stars in Andromeda lay far beyond those of the Milky Way that we even began to consider the reality of a galaxy other than our own.

Eventually we grew impatient with visible starlight and realized we could see even further into the universe and back in time if we measured other wavelengths in the electro-magnetic spectrum of light, like radio or gamma-rays. We built enormous dishes and antennae to catch them. We launched balloon-borne collectors into the earth's very atmosphere and, eventually, keen-eyed satellites even further and above and into outer space.

YET LIGHT

In the dark, at least where I live, the Milky Way still spangles across the night sky. Star-shine, moon-shine... there is so much light in the darkness when you stop to look—really look: the breathtaking arc of shooting star; the mesmerizing pulse and wave of the aurora borealis. The steely light of a full moon on a clear night can drip like quicksilver, painting everything pewter and pearl in the onyx night. There's even the evensong of eye-shine; of the deer that browses in the meadow as my late-arriving headlights sweep over the scene and I make my way past her toward the house. When I make it a point to go back out into the vesper meadow the deer have usually made their way to the safety of the hedgerows. But when I stand where they were moments before and turn my face up to the spinning firmament I am always rewarded with a sight beyond words. The vast sweep of the starry night sky makes me reconsider the dark, the light, and where each comes from.

"Time is what keeps the light from reaching us," the thirteenth-century mystic Meister Eckhart said, "There is no greater obstacle to God than time."[11] The prehistoric light of every night sky arrives upon the retinas of our eyes from a time before time. The farther away a star is in space, the farther back it is in time (and therefore the closer it is to whatever was in the beginning). If there are so many fossilized photons from the far off and long ago only just now arriving, it stands, then, that there is still other light that has not yet arrived from other suns burning in other galaxies even further away and ago...

And all their yet-light, yet to be.

We are still basking in the light of what we have come to call "the Big Bang," our eyes still taking in the afterglow of that infinite first light so many billions of years later. There are even stars that have long ago exhausted their stores of energy—burned out—yet since they burned so long ago and far away, and light requires time to traverse the distance between, the last bit of their relic light has not yet even reached our eyes. The sun has set nearly 150,000 times since Galileo first studied the infinite universe through a lens, and well over half-a-million times since Muhammad's night journey. For what reason could it possibly be that there are so many billions of points of light in the night sky, and so many million more so far away their light hasn't yet arrived, even traveling at 186,000 miles per second?

Really, what's a billion years compared to a fleeting moment?

While what we call "light" is actually an extremely narrow band in a much wider spectrum, there are all kinds of other forms of electromagnetic radiation our human eyes cannot detect ricocheting through the universe, from gamma rays and x-rays, to the ultraviolet and the infrared. In other words, darkness isn't all that dark. Light rays are always entering our planet's atmosphere, even if the millions and millions of optical rods and

---

11. In Tolle, *The Power of Now*, 53.

cones of our human eyes do not perceive them. The fact is that, although we depend upon our eyes to help us make sense of the world, they all too often deceive us. Perhaps that's why prophets from so many faith traditions speak of looking with the eyes of the heart. More than one mystic has wondered what good our eyes are to us, if our hearts are blind. When Meister Eckhart wrote, "The eye with which I see God is the same eye with which God sees me," he was not referring merely to the human eye, the physical organ of sight; rather, he was speaking metaphorically of the inner vision of the human heart.[12]

O HOLY NIGHT

It seems there's no getting away from the light—especially these days, when the lights are always on. Originally, though, before the ultraviolet hum or haze of fluorescent light bulbs or prescription sleep aids, our bodies understood something about darkness that our minds did not: We need the dark as much as the light. The circadian rhythm that modulates our sleeping and wakefulness depends on light and dark in right relationship, on a certain balance between sunlight and shadow.

The hours of darkness and those of daylight rise and fall in equal measures but twice a year, though, on our tilted planet: at the Spring and Autumn equinoxes. Every other day of the year we lean decidedly toward either more light or more darkness. It appears to be out of balance, but equal is different from equilibrium. Balance is not a static state, but a constantly changing way of adjustment and re-adjustment; a verb much more than a noun. Yet we tend to color our feelings light or dark, equate them with either night or day, and then assign them judgments like "good" or "bad." And it isn't as much a simple case of either/or as it is about one versus the other. We pit feeling against feeling, always tipping the scales in favor of whichever one we perceive to be more like the light. The mainstream view in our contemporary culture is to avoid having even the faintest hint of the blues at any cost. And, there's a pill for that. We blindly chase after and pledge our allegiance to the pursuit of happiness, but do we really even know what that is?

The so-called "simple" Prayer of Saint Francis—a powerful petition so many have struggled to embody over the years—asks that we may have the strength to sow light wherever there is darkness. But hidden in that

---

12. Meister Eckhart, *Sermons and Treatises*, 87.

prayer and the life of Francis, or the hagiography of any enlightened one for that matter, is the notion that where there is darkness, we must first get to know darkness; that instead of trying desperately to get out of the dark night of the soul as quickly as possible—or trying to avoid it altogether—we might linger there in order to reach a different kind of dawn. Indeed, the dark night is seldom singular, not something meant to be conquered and left behind once and for all, but rather an ongoing process that can deeply inform and shape the lifelight of our being.

The dark can bring worry or rest; insomnia and night terrors both thrive in the dark. So too do the dreams and nighttime inspirations that have inspired both scientists and sacred scripture writers alike, and awoken astronomers and artists and dreamers since time immemorial. But just as revolutionary and dangerous is the dawn: while our blood vessels are at their least elastic in the early morning, our blood pressure, cortisol hormone levels, and blood glucose levels all significantly and rapidly rise in order to wake our senses and bodies from sleep. We are as much a part of the night as it is of us. The very rhythms of our bodies' every function, including the ebb and flow of our emotional being, are hardwired to respond on a cellular level to the primal and daily liturgy of night becoming day and becoming night again. The circadian rhythm that regulates our waking and sleeping depends not only upon light, but also sure and steady darkness.

An ancient pulsar pulses in every cell of our bodies—yours, mine—the universe spinning inside each and every one of us.

Nothing ultimately stands between us and the farthest reaches of the cosmos in any dimension, whether spatial or temporal. We are in fact made of the same stuff of the expanding universe and contain the whole of everything that ever was and is, and all that is yet to be. The same atoms that form you and me were forged in the heart of some distant, long ago star. Hydrogen, oxygen, and nitrogen; carbon, phosphorus and iron; these building blocks of life as we know it all came from stars that lived and died long before the earth ever spun, tilted on its axis just so. When Joni Mitchell sang, "We are stardust . . ." she wasn't just being poetic. Every atom in the universe was birthed in a star and flung into space and time in a supernova explosion. Still, we are not merely lumps of billion-year-old carbon, but temporal beings bound to eternity.

"Every particle of the world is a mirror," wrote the Persian poet Mahmud Shabistari, "In each atom lies the blazing light of a thousand suns

Time, Twilight, and Eternity

...In the pupil of the eye, an endless heaven."[13] "Every leaf of grass is no less than the journey-work of the stars," Walt Whitman reminded.[14]

Not only are we stardust, we are entire solar systems; we are our own galaxies. One Hindu scripture likens our bodies to holy cities and our hearts to shrines "in the form of a lotus" within which:

> ...can be found a small space. This little space within the heart is as great as this vast universe. The heavens and the earth are there, and the sun and the moon and the stars; fire and lightening and wind are there, and all that now is and is not yet—all that is contained within it (Chandogya Upanishad 8:3).

We constantly constellate our lives with all sorts of moments passed and yet to be. Some eclipse others. But there remain a whole host of satellites that we allow into our orbit: asteroids of cynicism and comets of fear—or for that matter, any of life's debris with whose orbit we will inevitably periodically intersect. Each has its own gravitational pull. Like any shooting star, the tiniest speck of doubt can create an equally astronomical event; the meteor of loneliness can leave a long sad trail across the dark night sky of our spirits. So too can we reflect starlight like a full moon into an otherwise dark time.

We all too often associate, abdicate, or relegate prayer to the stars of religion and spirituality of our cosmos—to masters, mystics, and monks—but the reality is we all burn with the same elements. We need not be a scholar, saint, or scientist to use the rods and cones of our eyes to witness and wonder—to allow them to become reliquaries that receive the relic light of the universe and hold the holy fragments of the firmament. So too do compassionate hearts that contain all the heavens and the earth beat in each of our chests. Our opposable thumbs and uniquely human hands are meant for holding on to others.

Some stars are double and revolve around each other.

If we are made of the stuff of stars, it follows that our prayers must also be; that our intercessions are born out of the same interstellar nebulae of life's dust and stuff and particles. Like the relic light of a distant star that long ago burned up the last of its energy, swelled to become a supernova, then collapsed in upon itself to become a super dense ball of elements and matter, only to cool and cease to shine. Yet its relic light will still continue to

---

13. In Star, *Two Suns Rising*, 142.
14. From his poem, "Song of Myself" in *Leaves of Grass*, 50.

ricochet through time and space. So too can our prayers be like light arriving from a dark and distant space: like the prehistoric light of ancient suns, the fossilized photons from faraway and all the yet-light yet to arrive—to be.

Prayer travels as fast and as incomprehensibly as does light; by the time we see any evidence of it in our lives it has already been on its way to us for some time. Both the heat we feel on our skin and the light we sense on our closed eyelids as we turn and face the sun were created at the center of that star millions of years ago. How many eons that energy took to make its way up through the sun's half-million miles of roiling hydrogen and helium, who knows? But once flared out from the surface of that fiery furnace, it catapulted across the 93-million miles that separate us from the sun in just eight minutes.

Whether we started with a Big Bang, or with a word whispered into—prayed over—wild nothingness; by some First Cause or primeval atom or some cosmic singularity, we ultimately cannot separate light from dark. Our story is inextricably bound up with that of the stars—those that presently burn, as well as those that lived and died long before our planet ever circled its own star. There are prayers that burn like a white-hot star, and others that fold in on themselves, and still others that travel across time and space dispersing their very substance all along the way, seeding the universe with atoms of hope and the elemental grace of everything needed for creation to unfold—to begin again.

Always we begin again.

The planet spins, bearing us from sunlight to starshine and through the dark.

PART TWO

Lauds

First Light

Begin in the dark.

Begin with the leading edge of the planet turning ever closer to its blessed star and the sky drifting ever so slightly away from the deep darkness; a nearly imperceptible and gradual lightening from onyx to amethyst, from cobalt to lapis lazuli, to turquoise and tourmaline. In the beginning there is only silence, a holy hush—the entire universe listening for some sacred syllable. Then, from out of the silent spinning, a single tentative intonation pierces the dark and empty quiet.

Another note.

And then . . . a trill.

And then a flood of music: birdsong fills the air. With every lilting, leafy note the early morning sky leans another shade lighter; cerulean and cerise, sapphire and saffron.

The avian chorus rises—an incantatory canticle—and twilight dawns.

The day is always dawning somewhere on this spinning planet and there are very few places where it is not accompanied by an avian chorus. "Wake up!' is the challenge we hear not only in the anthem of the bright-eyed birds, but also from chanticleers of every tradition—from the Buddha and from Jesus; from the Hindu yogi and the Sufi poet. "The breeze at dawn has secrets to tell you," Rumi wrote, "do not go back to sleep."[1] "Where morning dawns . . . [God] calls forth songs of joy," proclaims the Hebrew Bible (Psalm 65:8). We do not merely turn daily toward a star and source of nuclear fire burning millions of miles away whose gravitational pull twirls us through space, but to the sun—our sun—an ever unfolding first light.

"Born of the one light, Eden saw play."[2]

---

1. Rumi, *The Essential Rumi*, 36.

2. A line from the popular hymn "Morning Has Broken" originally published in 1931 with words by Eleanor Farjeon and set to a traditional Scottish tune. The song is

Time, Twilight, and Eternity

As with the eventide, the morning twilight arrives by degrees and in three distinct phases—astronomical, nautical, and civil—yet the dawn is not simply the opposite or reverse of dusk. "If you would learn more, seek information from the birds of the air," the Hebrew Bible councils (Job 12:7). The dawn has long been simply "cockcrow," the daybreak announced by roosters long before we ever thought to ask which came first, the chicken or the egg? In fact, for many Jews, thanking Hashem for "giving the rooster the ability to distinguish between day and night and thereby being able to wake us up in the morning" is part of their daily prayers every dawn and one of the hundred blessings they say every day. Islam teaches that there are three sounds most beloved by Allah, namely: the voice of the one who reads the Holy Qur'an, the cry of anyone calling for forgiveness before the break of day, and the crowing of the rooster that wakes the faithful for *fajr*, or morning prayers.

As startling and predictable as daybreak is, it is never the same. There are occasionally those spectacular sunrises that the photographer seeks, the stirring horizons that have surely inspired painters and poets and playwrights alike. Yet quite often the sunrise is less theatrical, more subtle, and shows up least where one would expect it to be. There are mornings when the eastern horizon quietly and simply slides from plain old midnight to a less-than-memorable forget-me-not blue. But more often than not on such muted mornings, if I turn away from the gathering daylight and look in the opposite direction, I can watch the sun-struck mountain that rises to the west catch fire with a rosy glow—first shell pink, then coral, then a brilliant vermillion.

If I do not turn, I am still reminded by the sparrows: "Look, the light comes unbidden—given—every day."

Whenever I consider the regenerative miracle of dawn I also realize it isn't only here and now, a local phenomenon, but everywhere and all the time. Just as the dawn paints "my" mountain, so too does it color the nearby Green and White Mountains purple and orange beyond it, as well as the Blue Ridge Mountains and the whole long range of the Appalachians beyond that. The same sunrise tips with tinsel the tops of the Alpilles, where van Gogh famously painted the starry sky, and gilds the peaks of the Hindu Kush in Afghanistan, beneath which lay veins of that precious blue

---

perhaps more widely known by its pop music version released by Cat Stevens (Yusuf Islam after his religious conversion) on his album *Teaser and the Firecat* (Santa Monica: A&M Records, 1971).

pigment—lapis lazuli—which Vincent used as background to his whirling starry visions. Even further it decorates the great Drakensberg Mountains of South Africa, illuminates the sacred peaks of the Himalayas, and reaches over the Rwenzori Mountains (so high, it is said, they can pull down the moon).

Just as the same sun paints so many horizons the world over, so too does twilight fall on many eyes: the sun sets and rises not within any one set of religious—or even secular—beliefs, but over all of them. And though we may whisper a particular prayer in a particular manner to the rising or setting sun, we cannot claim its revelatory light as our own. One morning I awoke to a dawn chorus quite unfamiliar to my North American ears as I watched the sun rise over the Indian Ocean off the eastern coast of Africa. The rhythm of the surf and the daybreak adagio of the ibis and yellow-weaver birds interwove themselves with the call of the muezzin from the speakers atop the nearby mosque:

As-salatu Khayrun minan-nawm . . . La ilaha illa-Allah.

"It is better to pray than to sleep . . . There is no god but God."

Not unlike the light, which begins and ends in darkness, sound arrives from and returns to silence. The best time to hear and identify birds is, in fact, dawn, that thin threshold of dark night becoming daylight, because that is when their arias are usually most exuberant. According to ornithology, the science of studying birds, their chatter, chirps, and chirrs are simply about establishing or maintaining territory, about sourcing food or finding mates or reinforcing social status. Their vocal virtuosity proves nothing more and nothing less than their genetic fitness. Yet so many traditional belief systems also maintain that birds sing simply for the sheer joy of it and in order to greet the sun.

The urge to welcome the morning twilight seems inherent in us, too, as is our affinity for the birds who sing the sun up each dawn. It seems the winged ones have always been our messengers and harbingers and avatars, from the raven and dove that Noah sent to scope out the dry land after the flood (Gen 8:7–12) to the sacred stature of the eagle in so many Native American cultures. The Iroquois (along with many other indigenous cultures of North America) believe the hermit thrush received its flutelike tremulous twilight voice from the spirit world. The crane is a beloved and powerful symbol in Japanese myth, art, and folklore. And everyone knows the owl is wise, and the stork brings good luck—not to mention newborn bundles of joy. We all want to be as happy as a lark, as chipper as the morning sparrow.

In Islam the fact that birds are able to navigate "the atmosphere of the sky" without falling to the ground is held out as proof of God's existence and omnipotence (*The Qur'an*, an-Naḥl 16:79). The Buddha's voice is likened to bird song in one *Mahayana sutra*. The Holy Spirit was known as *An Geadh-Glas*—or "the wild goose"—to early Celtic Christians. And in the teachings of the Vedas, the Hindu who has awakened in all realms, whether of matter or spirit, is considered a *Paramahamsa*, or "supreme swan," after that bird's mastery of all three elements of land, water, and sky.

A divine voice sings through all creation, says one traditional Jewish prayer. "All religion, all our singing, is but one song," insisted Rumi.[3] Among the dearest holy writings of India is the poetic dialogue known as the Bhagavad Gita, literally "the song of God."

In the beginning there was silence.

Then, there was sound.

According to the Hindu Scriptures, that holy sound is the eternal syllable "Om." Everything, including all of the past, present, and future is contained in this one sacred sound. For Christians that sounded breath—that Word—is Jesus. The seers and prophets of Taoism are called *Sheng Jen*, or "those who hear the voice of the Absolute." In Mahayana Buddhism, the Sanskrit name of the Bodhisattva of Infinite Compassion is also interpreted as "the one who listens deeply to the sounds of the world."

Our fine-feathered friends are hardly confined to the realms of religion, mythology, and culture, though: science has long been fascinated by their every aspect, from the curve of their beaks to the size of their brains to the hollow bones that make their flight possible. Leonardo daVinci was obsessed with the owl's keen sense of sight and the exquisite structure of its wings. The finches of the Galapagos were what captivated Charles Darwin, the father of evolutionary theory. He wrote that birds "have strong affections . . . and a taste for the beautiful" and was convinced of an innate aesthetic sense within many species. Ever the consummate scientist, he still (anthropomorphically) distinguished bird song from other bird sound as "musical expression" and wrote rhapsodically of "the delight given by its melody."[4] The biologist Roger Payne, reflecting on his studies of bird song,

---

3. Rumi, *The Soul of Rumi*, 47.

4. See Darwin, *The Descent of Man*, 451; and Darwin, *The Expression of the Emotions*, 89–90, respectively.

as well as his now famous discovery that the watery depths of our planet resound with the hymns of humpbacks and other whales as they sing their way through the seas, wondered whether the entire universe was, in fact, composed of music: "Is it possible that the universe sings," he wondered...

"Is it possible that God is the song of the universe?"[5]

"Why do birds sing?" is yet another seemingly simple question we think we should easily be able to answer. But in order to do that we must first be able to say what we mean by "sing" and whether or not that is really what the birds are doing. Further, in order to know why birds sing we must be able to identify succinctly what music itself is: to be able to say where breath ends and ballad begins, and where the borders are between sound and song and syllable. And what if there is no purpose to the birds' abundant calls and coos, or no real reason other than sheer delight and joy? The question has always been (and the question Darwin didn't dare ask): For what practical use is the beautiful? For what reason should beauty—whether in a spectacular sunrise, or an iridescent feather, or an avian aria—prevail... survive the sifting process of evolution and time?

Or for that matter: Why beauty at all?

We call the sounds of the bird world music and song, but really they are meaningful speech and language in their own right—albeit a wordless language we've no hope of understanding. They might as well be speaking in tongues. It is tempting to think of the whistles and warbles birds make as simple signal and communication and leave it at that. Except where we so often seem tone-deaf and struggle to find the right key in life, they're consistently pitch-perfect; they enchant, inspire, and enthrall. Blithe spirits, they embody our wistful longing for the lyrical life and the soaring heavens above with full-throated ease. "For what are the voices of birds," the poet Robert Browning mused, "but words, our words, only so much more sweet?"[6] Birdsong reminded Emily Dickinson of winged hope, a feathered thing that sits and steadfastly sings in the soul.[7]

The cowbird has been recorded as using more than forty different notes, some so high our human ears cannot hear them; the male chaffinch may sing his song half-a-million times in just one spring. Bereft of their mate, some birds will plaintively sing their former partner's refrain of the

---

5. Payne, *Among Whales*, 167.
6. From Part IV, "Night," of his verse play "Pippa Passes" in *Selected Poems*, 166.
7. See Dickinson, *Collected Poems*, 22.

courtship song. The nightingale knows hundreds of love songs in its heart; the little brown thrasher, hundreds more.

"A bird does not sing because it has an answer—" says one Chinese proverb, "it sings because it has a song."

We've too long linked beauty with rarity and taught that the beautiful is something subjective, that beauty is in the eye of the beholder. Beauty is not rare but commonplace, everyday, and everywhere. We wake, if we wake, to beauty all around. We've done nothing to create that beauty; it comes unbidden—given—everywhere reborn anew every day. Perhaps the more meaningful question isn't why the birds sing every day but, rather, why we do not. "Every moment is a new arrival, a new bestowal," Rabbi Heschel reminded, "(Our) cardinal sin is in our failure not to sense the grandeur of every moment."[8]

We may never know what goes through those tiny little minds as the winged ones wake the sun with song; what extreme proportion of their bird brains is devoted to making beautiful music, and why. Nor can we possibly comprehend how such a slight wisp of weightless air can become, in the reliquary of a robin's ribcage, an opus and orchestra. Who knows? Maybe we've gotten it all wrong and birdsong is neither simple territorial claim nor some solar wake-up call, but a prayer to one of their own: a spectacular fire-bird that arcs across the sky and answers light to their song. Maybe the birds are an ancient congregation in an aboriginal religion and their avian chorus a holy antiphon in some carefully orchestrated liturgy.

First light is not a primordial moment from the dawn of time but a timeless re-awakening, an eternal morning. It is never the same sky twice, just as it is never the same day and we are never the same person today as we were or will be on any other day. Things change; times change.

We change.

We do not wake simply from somnolence but to something that never was before and never will be again. The question every first blush of every day asks us is: "What will you do with this day, this moment, this breath and beauty—this light and life?" Not yesterday's gifts or challenges, whatever they may have been, nor the promise of tomorrow's light, but this beautiful shining world right now, today.

Every dawn—and every dusk—is less a moment in time as it is a dialogue. And so we add our prayers to those of the birds; we each consecrate the daybreak with a "dawn prayer" of our own, and sing praise and say

---

8. Heschel, *The Wisdom*, 51.

First Light

thank-you each in our own way: the Jewish *shacharit*, the Hindu *gāyatrī mantra*, the Muslim *ṣalāt al-fajr*, the Christian *lauds* . . .

Bird song, heart song, universal song.

The Eternal Now

God called out in the middle of the night.

And young Samuel answered God, "*Hineini*"—Here I am (1 Sam 3:4–8).

(*Begin with a quivering mass of air molecules; with wave and frequency travelling more than a thousand feet every second.*)

Moses heard God on fire—speaking from the fire—and Moses responded by saying, "*Hineini*"—Here I am (Exod 3:4). An angel called out to Jacob in a dream, and Jacob answered, "*Hineini*"—Here I am (Gen 31:11). Another time God asked the unthinkable of Abraham: "*Hineini*," said the patriarch—Here I am (Gen 22).

(*Begin with miniscule bones and ultra-fine hairs inside our ears translating pitch and sound into message and meaning—into hearing. Begin with call and response—with ricochet and reverberation and echolocation—begin with vibrating vocal chords.*)

When Isaac was old and his eyes were so weak that he could no longer see, he called for Esau his eldest son and said to him, "My son." "*Hineini*," Esau answered (Gen 27:1). In the year that King Uzziah died, God asked, "Whom shall I send?" And Isaiah said, "*Hineini*"—"Here I am. Send me" (Isa 6:1–8).

This arrestingly brave and tender Hebrew word—*hineini*—is spoken from the heart several times in the Tanakh, the portion of the Bible many know as the Old Testament. More than a simple response to roll call— "present and accounted for"— it is said more often than not at a pivotal, life-changing, and challenging moment. It implies an openness and responsiveness on the part of the one speaking: not just "Here I am," but, rather, "Here I am, come what may— ready, willing, and able." While the Hebrew word does not appear in the New Testament, its holy message is literally and physically embodied by Jesus in the Gospels. And if Mary had not answered similarly—"let it be"—well, there would be no gospel to tell.[1]

Among the Five Pillars of Islam—*shahada*, (faith); *ṣalāt*, (daily prayer); *zakāt*, (charity and alms-giving); and *sawm*, (ritual fasting)—there is also the *Hajj*, or the commitment to make a pilgrimage to Mecca at least once within one's lifetime. If there is an anthem to the *Hajj* it is surely the *Talbiyah*, the prayer the faithful repeatedly invoke during their pilgrimage: *Labbaik! Allahumma, Labbaik!* "Here I am at Your service O Allah, Here I am!"

In the beginning was the word and the word was *hineini*:
Here I am . . .
Let it be.

BE HERE NOW

We might convince ourselves that we can measure time, but the moments of our lives are extraordinarily mysterious and deeply sacred. In between the past and future the present is always here, always arriving—something about to be—already and not yet. It's easy to forget this timeless dimension of our lives amidst the profane demands of our everyday existence, the buzzing, beeping, bleeping alarms of our workaday world. But really the notion that we can divide time into anything at all—a year, month, or day; an hour, minute, or second; the past, present, or future—is only that: a notion. For many aboriginal people the concepts of "past" or "future" are completely foreign; anything that isn't the present moment simply falls into the catch-all category of "not now."

Sometimes it really is "now or never."

Ultimately, we must erase time in order to experience the eternal; every moment can become eternity. The truth is we don't have the time. All we have is right now. Our today is all that really matters. "The past and future veil god from our sight," cautioned the Sufi poet Rumi, "burn up both of them with fire."[2]

Begin here.
Begin now.
The present moment is the foundation upon which all time and space rests—and rises.

---

1. In some translations Mary does, in fact, respond to the angel with the holy Hebrew word "*Hineini*"—Here I am, e.g., the Orthodox Jewish Bible (Luke 1:38).

2. In Tolle, *The Power of Now*, 53.

Time, Twilight, and Eternity

(Again)

Call it prayer or awareness, call it contemplation or mindfulness or attention, it only exists in the present moment: the timeless moment of the mystics, the eternal now. Not endless duration but timelessness—the opposite of time—an already-happened that is still happening and is always about to happen. Since the beginning of time, spiritual masters from every tradition have all pointed to the present as key, a moment that somehow exists outside of time and even beyond our vocabulary. "Before Abraham was . . . I am" (John 8:58) Jesus proclaims in the New Testament, breaking all laws of physics and grammar. Pressed for identifying details, God does not tell Moses "I was" or "I will be" but "I am" (Exod 3:14). And then goes on to say that the name "I am" is now and will be "forever" (Exod 3:15b). Biblical Hebrew, in fact, operates more in terms of perfect and imperfect rather than past, present and future; its verbs denote actions that have either been completed or not completed. When Moses asks the Holy Name, he is more accurately told "*Ehyeh asher Ehyeh*"—not "I am" so much as "I am not yet who I am not yet." Say nothing about creation still unfolding, God isn't even finished being and becoming God.

In the beginning was the Not-Even-Yet, yet to become.

Now may be all we have to hold on to, but we still wrestle with it like Jacob did the angel that called to him in the night. To say that the present moment is an angel we wrestle with is an understatement. If we're not busy recollecting, we're more often than not full of anticipation or worry. Still, we routinely hold out our arms as Time Past and Time Future each slip a sleeve of their stiffly starched straitjacket over our arms. At first we find the confinement oddly reassuring; we seldom notice the sound of the straps sliding through buckles.

In Hinduism, chronological time is considered an illusion. Everything, at every moment, is suffused with Brahman, with the fullness of being and the sacredness of all time. In Buddhism, this notion is found in the Zen attitude of walking the thin tight-rope of the present moment, and the understanding that in being fully present one is somehow both within and outside of time. The past and future held little opportunity for enlightenment to the poet T. S. Eliot; the still point of consciousness he sought could only be found outside of the usual definitions of time. "Before the beginning and after the end," he wrote, ". . . all is always now."[3]

---

3. The common theme of his interlinked poems known collectively as "Four Quartets" is our relationship with time, the universe, and the sacred. See Eliot, *Collected*

The Eternal Now

Thomas Merton reflected often on the present in his journals, on "the reality of now—the unreality of all the rest," as he put it.[4] Every moment is a portion of eternity—if only we are present enough to enter the moment (which then opens every other moment that ever was, is, or will be). Eternity, counter-intuitively, happens in the now. We think "now" is just a flash in the pan, a fleeting moment, a ridiculously short stretch of time. But really it is fathomless—infinite in every direction. The past is always past; the future always arriving, yet to be. But the present moment is always present.

It's always now. And will always be now forever.

Prayer, attention, and contemplation have long been the gateway into the eternal present moment, the "now that does not pass away," as Saint Augustine put it. "As for the present," he wrote, "should it be always present, and should it not pass into time past, time truly it could not be, but eternity."[5] The early Christian desert fathers and mothers spoke often of the importance of *agrupnia*, the discipline of attending to every moment, of spiritual "wakefulness." Saints in the tradition of Tibetan Buddhism called this practice "pure and total presence." In Hinduism, a similar way is called "witnessing." The French Jesuit priest Jean-Pierre de Caussade regarded the present moment as a profound sacrament.

What the Taoist teacher Lao-Tzu called "quieting the mind," the Hindu yogi Patanjali called "watching the breath." What Brother Lawrence calls "the little interior glance" in his time-honored Christian text, *Practice of the Presence of God*, the twentieth-century American Quaker Thomas Kelly calls "continuously renewed immediacy," in his equally classic *A Testament of Devotion*.[6] "The Now is no mere nodal point between past and future," he wrote, "It is the seat and region of the Divine Presence itself."[7]

Jesus is always reminding his disciples to be attentive, to stay watchful, and to be awake (Matt 25:13; Luke 12:37; Mark 13:33–37). In Sanskrit, the name "Buddha" means "I am awake." The Hindu concept of *moksha*; the Zen experience of *kenshō*; the Judeo-Christian idea of eternity; the Japanese understanding of *satori*, or awakening; the Muslim goal of *Jannah*, of entering into gardens of perpetual bliss; and the Buddhist philosophy of *nirvana* all resonate with this profound recognition that there is something

---

Poems, 175–208.

4. See, for example, *A Search for Solitude*, 214–215.
5. Augustine, *Confessions*, 215.
6. Kelly, *A Testament of Devotion*, 31.
7. Ibid., 95.

holy to be experienced in moment-by-moment attentiveness—in abiding in the ever abiding now.

YOU ARE HERE

Begin again; behold, be here . . . in this beautiful right now.

The ultimate representation of space is infinity; of time, eternity. Every sunrise is a bodhisattva of boundless space and infinite volumes of time, a reminder of both a tangible world of atoms, stars, and galaxies, as well as the immeasurable ground of meaning and mystery, beauty and consciousness. Sunrise and resurrection were synonymous in the eyes of the French novelist Victor Hugo; for the English poet Sir Henry Newbolt dawn was a kind of sacred wine. Just as many think of traditional sacraments,[8] every daybreak can also be an outward sign of an inward grace; an astronomical and everyday Eucharist—not just a sacrament of the present moment, but the sacrament of the broken day given to us to take, bless, break, and give: our daily bread.

"Whenever anyone seeks to loosen the chains of injustice, or share food with the hungry, clothe the naked, or provide shelter to those who wander, they will shine like the dawn," says Isaiah. If they call out to God for help, *God* will answer: "*Hineini*"—Here I am (Isa 58:6–9).

It has been said that we have two ears for a reason: that we might listen twice as much as we speak. Not only do we call out; we are called to every day.

(*Begin with music heard ever so intimately—so deeply—that we not only hear but become the music.*)

One of the dearest prayers I know of is to stand before the rising sun and say:

Labbaik Allahumma Labbaik . . .
Hineini . . .
Here I am.

---

8. For example, as the *Book of Common Prayer* puts it: "outward and visible signs of inward and spiritual grace, given by Christ as sure and certain means by which we receive that grace" (BCP 857–58).

House of Breath

Breathe in . . .

Breathe out . . .

We do it all the time. In fact, the average adult human at rest takes at least a dozen breaths every minute. Multiply those breaths by sixty for the minutes in an hour; then twenty-four for the hours in a day, and we breathe more than seventeen-thousand times from one sunrise or sunset to the next. Not that we're aware of even a fraction of those breaths; how our diaphragm and chest muscles work in concert with each other to pull air into our lungs, and how the bronchia and alveoli in our lungs retrieve oxygen from the trillions and trillions of air molecules contained in each breath, sending that precious element into our bloodstream where it circulates to and enlivens every cell of our bodies. We can survive for weeks without food; days without water. But take away our breath and we last only mere minutes.

Every moment is a house built out of breath within which we then abide, its walls functioning like lungs expanding and contracting. We create every one of our days out of thin air, moments in time that literally inspire.

But what exactly is it that we breathe?

What is it that truly sustains us?

We know now about things like the precious presence of oxygen in the atmosphere of this third planet from the sun in a cosmos of other suns and planets and galaxies composed of other gases and elements. But this wasn't always the case. For centuries air was thought to be a pure element in and of itself. In the 1770s the Swedish chemist Carl Scheele experimented with what was certainly oxygen, but which he called "fire-air." One seventeenth-century scientist wrote in his wonderfully titled book, *Suspicions about the Hidden Realities of Air*: "I have often suspected that there may be in the Air some yet more latent Qualities or Powers . . . . For this is not as many imagine a simple and elementary body, but a confused aggregate."[1] The first to coin the word for the invisible, life-sustaining particles of the air we breathe was a French scientist, Antoine Lavoisier, who named it "oxygène" in his native tongue sometime late in the eighteenth century.

A breath can be the air physically inhaled and exhaled in the act of respiration—our ceaseless search for oxygen; or it can be a momentary pause or rest; the tiniest trace or suggestion of something else; a slight breeze in the air; a delicate whisper. Or it can be the spirit, essence, and vitality of life itself: our very soul. Stand before extraordinary beauty—a spectacular sunset, say—and we say it takes our breath away. A breath of fresh air isn't welcome only for its oxygenation, but for the welcome change it can bring whenever we feel stuck or stale or stagnant. Similarly, when we need to take a break from something, we say we need to take a breather, or we need to catch our breath. We waste our breath on the unyielding or hopeless; we hold our breath in anxiety or expectation. Or if we're feeling particularly amorous we might even say that love is in the air.

Take a deep breath—begin again.

Our lungs are not the only organs capable of extracting oxygen from the air; our eyes can breathe, too. Cells on the surface of our eyes can absorb tiny bits of oxygen directly from the atmosphere in addition to receiving the regular portion supplied by the more traditional route of oxygenated blood carried throughout the body via blood vessels. With each flutter of our eyelids our eyes not only drink in great gulps of light but take a deep breath of sky. In fact, the beauty of every sunrise and sunset sustains life as we know it. Every day the planet itself breathes: the deep in-breath of sunlight arriving with the dawn warming the earth and increasing oxygen levels in the atmosphere, and the equivalent exhalation of sunlight's departure at dusk cooling the planet and suppressing the production of oxygen.

UNIVERSAL: BREATH

In so many languages the word for "spirit" or "soul" seems to have been literally inspired by the word for "breath." The Latin *spiritus*, for example, can mean "breath," but also "life-force," or even "vigor," and is the source from which the English word "spirit" is derived. The most frequent translation of the Greek *pneúma* as it appears in the New Testament is "spirit," although it can also mean "wind" or "breath." Similarly, the Hebrew word

---

1. Robert Boyle, in Stager, *Your Atomic Self*, 15.

rûach is synonymous with "spirit," "breath," and "wind." Indeed, *rûach* is the primordial breath, the divine wind of the Creator blowing over what was to become:

> In the beginning God created *hashomayim* (the heavens) and *haaretz* (the earth). And the earth was *tohu vavohu* (without form, and void); and darkness was upon the face of the deep. And the *Rûach Elohim* was hovering upon the face of the waters" (Gen 1:1–2, OJB).[2]

(Even twilight is inspired in Hebrew: *Nesheph*, a word used to denote "twilight" in the Hebrew Bible, is more properly defined as the time "when the evening or morning breeze blows.")[3] The entire universe is, according to Hebrew tradition, dependent upon the continual outflow of *Rûach Elohim*, the divine breath that not only breaths but speaks it into existence.

All things vibrate with divine breath. "God is the breath inside the breath," wrote the fifteenth-century Indian mystic poet Kabir.[4] *Atman*, the self or soul; *Brahman*, or absolute Reality; and the breath are intimately connected throughout the ancient scriptures of India, where in the Upanishads spirit is associated with *prana*, a Sanskrit word which can mean "life-force" but also "breath." The creator god of the Creek Indians is known as the Master of the Breath, the one who sends the winds that direct the destiny of the people. The Navajo speak of *nilch'i*, meaning not only wind and air, but also that which gives life. The Lakota honor *Woniya wakan*, or the holy air, in their ceremonies. One Zuni legend speaks of how the great ancestors came out of the world before this one and, upon seeing the Sun Father, took a deep breath of that holy light.

Everywhere around the planet we depend on something invisible and elemental which enters into us and nourishes us from within for our very existence. So many traditions hold that their sacred scriptures are "living texts." In other words: they breathe. Jesus is considered to be the incarnate Word of God; the Holy Qur'an is said to have been uttered directly

---

2. While the relevant term in the opening of the Torah is commonly translated into English as "the Spirit of God was hovering over the waters ..." a more direct rendering of the Hebrew *Rûach Elohim* could be: "a wind from God," or even "the breath of God," a translation favored in many authoritative English translations of the Hebrew Bible from its original.

3. E.g. in the original Hebrew, ". . . at twilight, as the day was fading" (Prov 7:9), and "At dusk they got up . . ." (2 Kgs 7:5), the word translated to "twilight" and "dusk" is *nesheph*. The same word is also translated to "dawn" in Job 7:4 and Psalm 119:147.

4. Kabir, *Ecstatic Poems*, 45.

from Allah in one breath. Indeed, breath is as intrinsically intertwined with speech and words as it is with spirit; and divine speech even further, albeit far beyond anything conceivable by human thought.

Our speechless wonder and our words, it seems, are inextricably interwoven: as early as Aristotle, one of the first terms for "butterfly" was the Greek word *psyche*; a word that has also been associated with both "breath" and "soul."

Breath by breath—cell by cell—we are all radically becoming, transforming into someone and something else; not entirely new, and yet still neither completely finished nor past. Nothing stands still or remains the same. Including us. Over the span of our lifetimes every one of the skin cells with which we were born will have been sloughed off and replaced by entirely new cells. With every exhalation we scatter bits and pieces of us to the wind; with every in-breath we incorporate new "star-stuff" into that part of the universe we call our body. "What is called birth is change from what we were—and death the shape of the old left behind," the poet Ovid wondered in his *Metamorphoses*, "How many creatures walking on this earth have their first being in another form?"[5]

And yet we are not worms, not caterpillars metamorphosing into butterflies. Still, there cannot be one without the other, an after without a before—and all the consequent implications of not only the passage of time, but the notion that what came before was not-the-same, not-enough, incomplete, or insufficient. The true miracle of every metamorphosis is neither the butterfly nor the caterpillar imagining something else, something beyond; but the instar and the chrysalis.

What matters is the in-between.

There is an eternal echo of the spinning worm having turned itself inside-out in the twice-daily metamorphosis of night becoming day and day becoming night. The possibility of our truest form is held out every day, every moment. We can no sooner fully fit ourselves back into before than the butterfly, having unfurled its wings, can return to its shed skin or its chrysalis.

Nothing stands still or is permanent. With every breath we can begin again, anew.

(Amen.)

But impermanence, at least from the perspective of what the Buddha taught, is not the same as annihilation; just as emptiness is not nothingness.

---

5. Ovid, *The Metamorphoses*, 425–426.

"Impermanence means being transformed at every moment."[6] This is also the manner in which so many Eastern mystics approach matter: that we are a part of nature and nature is never static. As one Taoist text puts it:

> The stillness in stillness is not the real stillness. Only when there is stillness in movement can the spiritual rhythm appear which pervades heaven and earth . . . . To change with change is the changeless state.[7]

Begin with a breath: this one.
Begin with a word: "here" . . . another: "now."
Begin with extraordinary life all around, everywhere, and everywhen.

The notion of sacred scripture as a living, breathing reality is perhaps nowhere more explicit than in the Jewish tradition, where it is thought that not only scripture as a whole but the individual letters comprising it are alive. Because the Ten Commandments are believed to have been dictated to Moses directly by God, the letters of that sacred text—the twenty-two letters which also comprise the Hebrew *aleph-beth*, or "alphabet"—are considered to be themselves actual traces of divine speech. Indeed, it was by combining these same letters into such primal utterances as: "Let there be lights in the vault of the sky to separate the day from the night, and let them serve as signs to mark sacred times, and days, and years . . ." (Gen 1: 14) that the visible universe and the here and now are here at all.

Both the word and the world are created from letters; not so much having been spoken, but being spoken—breathed—into each and every sunset and sunrise as the planet spins, tilted on its axis just so. The world was not created—past tense; its creation occurs every day. Some would even say with every breath. The twilit sky only exists because it is still being spoken into reality. The letters of God's first alphabet are still there lighting up the heavens and upholding the entire universe. Every dawn, existence itself says "Let there be light!"

Begin again.

Sacred among the Hebrew names for God is the Tetragrammaton, the four-letter name, YHWH (*Yod, Heh, Vav, Heh*), often written out in non-Hebrew texts as "Yahweh" or even "Jehovah." Thought to be unpronounceable—or unspeakable; not to be pronounced—Jews have long substituted many other names for the divine: *Elohim* ("God"), *HaShem* ("The Name"),

---

6. Hanh, *No Death, No Fear*, 47.

7. Hong Zicheng, an ancient Chinese sage who combined Confucian, Taoist, and Buddhist teachings. See Robert Aiken's translation of Zicheng's *Caigentan*.

or *Adonai* (My Lord), among them. As it turns out, many are convinced the most holy name was not and is not meant to be pronounced or spoken at all, but breathed: the sacred sound of the ultimate inhalation (*YH*) and exhalation (*WH*).[8] That the letters of God's name are comprised of what every one of us does every moment of our days and all the time whether it is dusk or dawn, night or day: the autonomic acts of breathing in . . .

. . . and breathing out.

This makes God the first and last word on our lips—and prayer our constant state—from the first light of our first day to the twilight of our last.

BREATHING TIME

In the language of many Sufi scriptures, the word for breath is associated not only with spirit but also with time; the Persian word *dam* can mean either "breath" or "moment." Thus, "*Hush dar dam*," the first of several principles in Naqshbandi Sufism, is understood as "awareness in the breath," and "awareness in the moment." Breath is the foundation of our spiritual home; not only in the in-breath and out-breath, but in the in-between moment between the two, when many believe the soul, in that split-second, returns home. "The more that one is able to be conscious of one's breathing, the stronger is one's inner life," taught Bahâ ad-Dîn Naqshband, "It is a must for everyone to safeguard [the] breath in the time of . . . inhalation and exhalation and further, to safeguard [the] breath in the interval between the inhalation and exhalation."[9]

The direction to follow each breath, to pay attention to our every breath, has been the key so many spiritual paths and teachers have urged when it comes to unlocking the mysteries of our yearning and restless soul, of mindfulness and prayer. It turns out they were right all along:

We all take in great breaths of God—all the time.

The truth is our every breath is prayer. We all "pray without ceasing" (1 Thess 5:16–18), whether we're aware of it or not—at least seventeen-thousand times a day.

If we follow our breath long enough we can end up back at the beginning of time. We all share the same air—and not just us here and now, but those who breathed before us and those who will breath after us. While most, if not all of the oxygen molecules in any one of our breaths are

---

8. See, for example, Abram, *The Spell of the Sensuous*, 249–50.
9. In Vaughan-Lee, *Love Is a Fire*, 173.

relatively unstable and linger only briefly in the atmosphere before they are dispersed or absorbed or transformed into vapor or carbon dioxide (CO_2) or some other compound, there are other particles in the air we breathe that have been around for quite some time. The ancient and persistent atoms of argon in the atmosphere, for example, can come pretty close to measuring time in terms of eternity. While argon is present in the air all around us, it is of no beneficial use to us; we simply inhale it along with the rest of the atmospheric gases in our quest for oxygen—and get rid of it, along with CO_2 in our very next exhalation. One astronomer, Harlow Shapley, famously followed the argon atoms in a single breath. "Every saint and every sinner of earlier days, and every common man and common beast," he concluded, "have put argon atoms into the general atmospheric treasury." Our next breath, according to Shapley, might contain "more than 400,000 of the argon atoms that Gandhi breathed in his long life."[10]

It is entirely possibly that argon atoms from the time of Abraham are still floating around in the atmosphere. With our next breath, we might inhale the same bit of air as the Buddha breathed beneath the Bodhi Tree; or the last earthly breath of Jesus as he hung on the cross at Golgotha. The same breath as Galileo breathed as he gasped in amazement and awe before the sight of the universe in his spyglass. The frozen sighs of Vincent van Gogh as he looked up in the chill of a starry, starry night . . . Who knows? Maybe even the same breath ever breathed into the very first human.

"Every atom belonging to me as good belongs to you."[11]

A NEW HEAVEN AND A NEW EARTH

We are not only sustained by each breath we take; we are, in a very real way born again and anew. Resurrection does not happen in the by-and-by, but in the here-and-now. The true source of liberation, Buddha taught, is our ability to be in the present moment wisely and earnestly. "Can any one of you by worrying add a single hour to your life?" Jesus asks in the Gospel according to Matthew (6:27). Past regrets and future fears require time; they cannot survive in the timelessness that is right now—the present moment—which is as close and accessible as the very next breath we take. This is the kind of "spiritual respiration" that John Wesley, co-founder of Methodism, preached about: "God's breathing into the soul, and the soul's

---

10. Shapley, *Beyond the Observatory*, 48–49.
11. Whitman, *Leaves of Grass*, 25.

breathing back what it first receives from God; a continual action upon the soul, the re-action of the soul upon God; an unceasing presence. . ."[12] And the same phenomenon and practice that, centuries later, contemporary Buddhist teacher Thích Nhất Hanh has referred to as a kind of resurrection—that when we are fully present in the present moment we are outside of time and actually and already within the Pure Land of Buddha, the Sabbath Eternal, the Heavenly Paradise, and the Kingdom of God:

> Our practice is always to resurrect ourselves, going back to the mind and the body with the help of mindful breathing . . . This will produce our true presence in the here and now. Then we can become alive again . . . . Whether you eat or drink or breathe or walk or sit, you can practice resurrection. Always allow yourself to be established in the here and now—fully present, fully alive. That is the real practice of resurrection.[13]

Every morning the day is reborn; every moment is a new beginning. When this finally dawns on us it is possible for every sunrise and sunset to paint the skies not only of the heavens beyond us, but also those in the beyond that is within us—where everything that has ever been since time's beginning, is now, and ever will be is always just beginning: the twilight of a new dawn. "What a day today," Rumi wrote of that kind of awakening and moment, "There are two suns rising! . . . Oh, you who can see into your own heart."[14]

In the end there is no eschatology; only breath—exhalation and inhalation; only heartbeat—systole and diastole.

Only renewal and return.

In all three Abrahamic faiths there is a belief in a future messianic era that will usher in a time of justice and peace, even if the understanding of "messiah" differs greatly between them. Christians believe in the second coming—the return—of Christ. In Islam there will come *al-sā'ah*, or the Hour, when a prophesied redeemer will return accompanied by Jesus to liberate believers and return the world to serenity before the (hoped-for) Day of Resurrection. In Judaism the Prophet Elijah will return to herald the Messiah who will, amongst other things, return the Jewish people to the Holy Land and all mankind to the Garden of Eden. In Buddhism the bodhisattva Maitreya will return and guide the entire cosmos into nirvana.

---

12. Wesley, *The Works of John Wesley*, 1:442.
13. Hanh, *No Death, No Fear*, 98–99.
14. In Star, *Two Suns Rising*, xi.

Shiva and Vishnu return in the form of the avatar Kalki in the long cycle of Hindu time and the universe will dissolve and regenerate anew.

The planet spins, the moon circles, tides rise and fall, and seasons come and go.

The sun sets—and rises. . .

Time after time.

The scientific facts appear to indicate that the universe will likely expand into infinity and eternity—a single long exhalation into vast space and stretching over eons and eras and incomprehensibly long periods of time as we know it—galaxies drifting ever further away and apart until there is nothing left but infinite darkness. But what if the story does not end there? Perhaps, as some astronomers believe, some overarching force will counteract the expansion first set in place by the Big Bang and pull the outward-moving universe back together again. Call it the cosmos collapsing in upon itself; call it a whimper, the opposite of the Big Bang; call it gravity . . .

Or call it God breathing back in.

And after that?

Who knows—none of us do, really—perhaps the universe will return to void and nothingness, to the chaos from which our own present universe was birthed.

Or maybe God will take another long holy breath and there will be "a new heaven and a new earth" (Rev 21:1).

The Fullness of Time

Our constant prayer may be for more time—just one more minute—but in the big picture all we really have is right now, a time we ultimately cannot divide up and measure out, but simply pours into us, fills us to overflowing, and flows back out into the world. The good news? It is always right now. Time and eternity constantly join together in the present moment—in the fullness of time, to use that prophetic biblical phrase. In the fullness of time we have more than enough, we have plenty of time . . . we have time on our hands.

"Everything has its time," the Hebrew Bible proclaims, "For everything there is a season, and a time for every matter under heaven" (Eccl 3:1, NRSV). Really, the only time we can say exists at all is this moment, the one that just now flew by. The present moment is thought to last approximately three seconds in our human minds according to the present-minded psychologists and neuroscientists who study such things. That's a single slippery second for each letter of that little three-letter wonder: *n-o-w*. The trouble is, by the time the last second of that slimmest syllable of time ever makes its way into our consciousness, the present has inevitably already begun to slide into its shifty old habit of becoming *then*. (It was, after all, a whole two seconds ago.) Now then, we know now and then are not the same; it's just that—well, for the time being, being in time is our only choice.

Unless it isn't, and we've gotten it wrong all this time.

In the native tongue of the Mi'kmaq people, the present moment lasts for more than one syllable: *neegah* is their "now." They have no words for clock time, for hour or minute or second, as is the case in so many aboriginal cultures. In Inuit "now" is *koviashuvik*, five syllables worth of "living in the present moment with quiet joy and happiness." In French, though, "now" is *maintenant*, which adds up to a ten-letter wonder and begs the

The Fullness of Time

question (along with *neegah* and *koviashuvik*) of whether the present lasts longer if you experience it in another place, another culture or language.

A beautiful word in a beautiful language, *maintenant* not only means "now," but is time that we can, uncharacteristically, hold on to: etymologically, it is derived from the French words for "hand" and "to hold, or possess." Time held in the hand—*maintenant*—a lovely embodiment of William Blake's image of heaven:

> To see a world in a grain of sand
> And heaven in a wildflower
> Hold infinity in the palm of your hand
> And eternity in an hour.[1]

In a very real way neither the future nor the past exists, at least not right now. So too can we say that the only moment in which we are real is this one. Try as we might, we can no sooner physically transport ourselves into the future as we can return ourselves to the past. The only place and time we really can be is here and now. And yet simply having been here we all have a past and we're all tempted by the future.

How can we not be?

It seems impossible not to have at least one eye if not both fixed on the future these days. In this lead-follow-or-get-out-of-the-way world there is no room for lingering in the moment. We ask each other, motivationally, where we see ourselves five years from now; we draft specific and strategic ten-year plans. Meanwhile we seldom take the time to notice where we are right now. The future arrives alarmingly fast: five years, ten . . . fly by before we even have time to file those plans in our "To do" file. If we don't tie our lives to the next quarterly report, we focus on some other aspect of the calendar—or worse, fiscal—year. We do everything "by the clock."

Today, with all our digital doo-dahs and devices, we're always trying to keep up with time. Yet none of these have anything to do with real time or the natural rhythms of the universe, and therefore real life. We know and experience nothing like "the fullness of time" (Gal 4:4; Eph 1:9–10) Saint Paul and others wrote of so long ago and still today—from St. Augustine's *nunc stans*, "the now that does not pass away," to Thích Nhât Hanh's *Present Moment Wonderful Moment*, or even the poet Rilke's understanding that "What lingers / is what truly consecrates."[2]

---

1. The oft-quoted opening lines of his poem "Auguries of Innocence." See *The Complete Poetry*, 490.

2. See also Hahn, *Inside the Now*. The line from Rilke comes from one his "Sonnets

We know only time's emptiness.

This isn't to say that we ought to completely abandon clock-watching and calendar planning and page turning, or turn our backs on the time-sensitive matters of daily life. We need not become oblivious to time's passing. It's just that in our 24/7 world we seem to have forgotten that in addition to knowing what time it is we need to know what kind of time it is. It takes vigilant attention to remain in the present moment for even a moment, something the desert fathers understood all too well. While they practiced *agrupnia*, the discipline of attending to every moment, Abba John Climacus urged his brothers and sisters to resist the arch-enemy of that attentiveness: *anesthesia*, the thoughtlessness that numbs us to the sacredness of time; dulls our sense of time—of us—becoming ready, ripening every moment.

Yet we can neither see nor touch time—its arrival, presence, or departure. It has no color, flavor, sound, or texture other than those we assign to and associate with it.

Or can we?

MOUTH-WATERING TIME

The American essayist and poet Ralph Waldo Emmerson, who led the Transcendentalist movement of the mid-nineteenth century, noted in his diary that his contemporary, Henry David Thoreau, told time neither by the sun nor the clock or calendar, but botanically:

> On the day I speak of he looked for the *Menyanthes*, detected it across the wide pool, and, on examination of the florets, decided that it had been in flower five days. He drew out of his breast-pocket his diary, and read the names of all the plants that should bloom on this day, whereof he kept account as a banker when his notes fall due: The *Cypripedium* not due till to-morrow. He thought that, if waked up from a trance, in this swamp, he could tell by the plants what time of the year it was within two days.[3]

Once upon a time we all told time by what was ripe in the forest or field or, even closer to home, in the garden. Tender stalks of asparagus and bunches of wild dandelion leaves heralded spring; apples only snapped in

---

to Orpheus" in *Prayers of a Young Poet*, 15.

3. In Thoreau, *The Winged Life*, 78.

The Fullness of Time

the crisp autumn air (unless, of course, they were drunk in the form of hard cider to lighten up the dark days of winter.) Summer days were measured by what berry was ripe, and everyone understood the subtle difference between those succulent first moments of strawberry and the last glowing moments of blueberry, when the little jewels burned incandescent in the late summer sun. Everyone waited with anticipation for the first bite of sweet corn, some yielding to temptation and wading out into the field to shuck an ear right off the stalk, strip off husk and silk, and bite into those tender, milky-sweet kernels.[4]

Not all of us have forgotten that time ticks to a natural rhythm. The morning or evening calls of birds continue to announce the hour from Papua New Guinea to the raucous rooster up the road. Around the globe many people still retain and consult a calendar of fruits or flowers, figuring where they are in the year according to what is ripe or blossoming; tasting what time it is, smelling the scent of each savory second.

One imaginative Frenchman, Monsieur de Villayer, went so far as to invent a spice clock. Waking before daybreak in the seventeenth century, after the invention of the clock but before the invention of the lightbulb, meant not being able to see what hour it was. De Villayer developed a special clock on which each nighttime hour had a little depression containing a different and easily distinguishable spice. When he woke in the night he could simply feel his way to whichever spice the hour hand was pointing, dip his finger into that hour's flavoring, and smell or taste what time it was without the bother of getting up to light a candle in order to see what time it was (waking up at, say, half-past cardamom, or falling back asleep to the nutmeg hour).[5]

It is, gloriously, summer as I write these words; August to be exact. My daily walk took longer than usual this morning as I stopped to revel in, gather, and eat the wild blueberries ripening in the lower meadow. In my journal I simply noted it was "8/2." But that numerical shorthand for the calendar day, or even its lengthier version—"the second day of the eight month"—reflects nothing of my meadowland morning. How the sunlight was more golden, less blue than when I snow-shoed here last February; or how different the air smelled; or how today the field is brilliantly dotted

---

4. I have explored this notion of seasonality and ripening time elsewhere. See *Blueberry Fool*, especially, pp.34–35.

5. De Villayer's spice clock is detailed in Cipolla, *Clocks and Culture*, 69; and, Boorstin, *The Discoverers*, 36.

indigo; or that, in fact, I could taste what time of year it was. I had not merely arrived in the blueberry meadow in chronological, calendric time, but in a time made miraculously ripe, ready, and full: a kairos moment. This past winter's snowmelt had watered the roots of those wild plants, and the spring sun slowly warmed the earth around them, coaxing both leaf-bud and blossom from barren twig so that, in turn, the bumblebees could pollinate each waxy white flower bell. Then, all season the summer days embraced them, growing them into starry-eyed berries and ripening them until they—and I—finally arrived at this morning's perfect blue hour, that mouth-watering moment in the meadow.

THE TIME IS RIPE

In the original first drafts of the poems that would eventually come to be published as *The Book of Hours*, the poet Rilke included short annotations that not only dated their composition, but also described what else was going on in his exterior as well as interior landscape. Thus, a poem might be dated: "On the 20th of September in the evening hour after a lengthy rainstorm, when the sun suddenly broke through the forest's dark canopy and through me," or, on the 26th of September "toward evening [when] there was hardly enough light shining upon this world to see the radiance playing upon the wet leaves of the blood-red, withering vine," or, more directly, "On the 29th of September, after fearful nights."[6] Again, this is less about knowing what time it is and more about understanding what kind of time it is.

That beautiful biblical phrase, "in the fullness of time," is used to describe a kairos moment when time is ripe. A time of completeness and promises fulfilled—just the right time, a time that had finally and fully come and yet does not come nor can be measured according to any mechanical, man-made clock. Both the Hebrew Bible and the New Testament declare that what to us appears to be a day is a thousand years to God, and a thousand years with God but a day (Ps 90:4; 2 Pet 3:8–9). What then do we make of our human lifetimes, our meager seventy or eighty or more, if we're lucky, years? We are born, we play and learn and grow into young men and

---

6. These notations were ultimately eliminated from the collection of poems Rilke initially referred to as *die Gebete*, or "the Prayers" and finally published as the first part of *The Book of Hours*. The quotes here are from Mark S. Burrows' lovely translation, *Prayers of a Young Poet*, pp. 35, 61, and 74.

women. We work and we toil, and we endure challenges and weep and we laugh. We learn how to love—and how to say goodbye. We ripen into old age. The sun rises and sets as surely as our hours rise and fall; the seasons of our spinning world—the seasons of our lives—rise and fall.

We rise and fall.

All in the blink of the universe's eye.

"Even when we don't desire: / God ripens."[7] For Rilke, God was not only 'the one who has been coming, the one imminent for an eternity, the future one," but also "the finite fruit of a tree on which we are the leaves."[8] In other words, we sustain Creation as much as Creation sustains us. When we pay careful attention to time we ripen the moment and time then becomes something sumptuous, tender, complete, lush, and abundant—in a word: *full*.

If we are ripening fruit, taught one Sufi mystic, "Muhammad is the juice; God is the taste."[9] The truth is time is always ripe for something, even if that something is simply being. "Now is the time!" every great teacher has proclaimed. We can consider every moment a step into eternity. "When you live in the now," Thích Nhât Hanh observes, "you see that your being can be limited neither by the space of a physical body nor by the time of a life span."[10] "See, now is the acceptable time," Saint Paul wrote, "see, now is the day of salvation!" (2 Cor 6:2b).

Everything is ready. Nothing stands still.

Begin again; be here and now—*maintenant*. Begin with time held in the hand like a luscious ripe fruit. Take a bite of now; sink your teeth into the present moment. Let time's sweet juice drip lavishly down your chin.

---

7. Ibid., 50.
8. Rilke, *Letters to a Young Poet*, 60.
9. Bawa Muhaiyaddeen in Barks and Green, *The Illuminated Prayer*, 61.
10. Hanh, *Inside the Now*, 147.

AFTER

Afterglow

The colors of the twilight sky vary from day to day. Not every sunrise paints a rosy picture; sunset can sometimes be the furthest thing from romantic. While so many sky-watchers—myself included—can imagine all sorts of messages in the twin twilights of each day, any sunrise or sunset is ultimately and only a random reflection of light entering the atmosphere at a certain angle: a combination of any given day's accumulation of dust and clouds, and other natural phenomenon. After a volcano violently erupted on a small Indonesian island in 1883, jettisoning billions of tons of ash and debris high into the stratosphere, the twilit skies around the globe glowed for months. Nearly forty-thousand lives, more than a hundred villages, and the main port of Anjer were lost in a matter of moments. Meanwhile, a vast cloud of volcanic ash began to circle the earth creating spectacular sunsets from horizon to horizon.

The "remarkable sunsets" of Krakatoa, as those virulent skies became known, did not go unnoticed; poets, painters, and scientists all responded to the unearthly drama and celestial display. The painter William Ascroft spent evening after evening trying to capture in pastel sketches the volcanic sunsets over the River Thames at Chelsea, making upwards of five-hundred studies in the gloaming. The Victorian poets Algernon Swinburne, Robert Bridges, and Alfred Tennyson all composed lines in homage to the "blood-red" skies of the spectacular sunsets of the 1880s.[1]

But it was the poet Gerard Manley Hopkins who, before the true cause of the atmospheric displays was ascertained—and before the world recognized the greatness of his poetry—wrote most widely on the atmospheric phenomenon sweeping over the earth. Hopkins did not live long enough

---

1. See Altick, "Four Victorian Poets" 249–60; and further Flint, *The Victorians and the Visual Imagination*, 57–58.

to bask in the light of his poetry shone into the world—"like shining from shook foil"[2]—almost all of the Jesuit priest's poems remained unpublished until well after his death. While his poetic life is entirely posthumous, several of his prose pieces were, however, published in his lifetime, all of them having to do with curious events in the sky.[3]

Volcanic twilights are now more widely studied and understood. Scientists have even given an official name—afterglow—to the atmospheric phenomenon produced by ash and dust particles and droplets of sulfuric acid lofted high into the troposphere and stratosphere after a volcanic eruption. But for the Victorians the apocalyptic hues of the lilac-, green-, and rose-damasked skies were curious if not unsettling. The sky was on fire: "more like inflamed flesh than the lucid reds of ordinary sunsets," Hopkins wrote. While we might know a little something more about the optics of sunlight falling through the atmosphere and the geology of volcanic eruptions today, people around the globe still fall to their knees before both the stunningly beautiful as well as the catastrophic.

Indeed, the line separating the two isn't always as distinct as we'd prefer it to be.

We've always read into the natural world and wondered why something is the way it is. More to the point, we wonder especially in trying times where God is. And at least as far back as Noah and Moses and Elijah, the answer has always been "after." All alone on Mount Horeb, Elijah heard the wind begin to howl in the middle of the night, and the ground shook, and the earth burned as if on fire. Elijah assumed that God, being so powerful, was surely in all that wind and shaking and burning. But God was not in the wind. And after the wind God was neither in the earthquake, nor after the earthquake in the fire. But *after* the fire . . .

". . . *after* the fire came a gentle whisper" (1 Kgs 19:11–12).

What any priest or prophet will tell you is that if you contemplate God long enough something shifts inside you. What neuroscientists have documented is that when we pray our brain physically changes. New synaptic

---

2. "The world is charged with the grandeur of God / It will flame out, like shining from shook foil. . . ." he wrote in an oft-cited line of his poem "God's Grandeur." See Hopkins, *The Major Works*, 128.

3. Several letters written by Hopkins were published in *Nature*, one of the leading scientific journals of his day. His first published letter, "A Curious Halo" (1882), detailed cloud-shadows opposite the setting sun and appeared before the Krakatoa sunsets; his essay, "The Remarkable Sunsets," was published in 1884, following the volcanic eruption. See further *The Correspondence*, 161–6.

connections are created and different neural pathways laid down. Areas of the brain governing social interaction, and therefore our capacity for empathy and compassion, are strengthened—which in turn fosters alterations in our perception and deepens our thoughtfulness. "If God has meaning for you, then God becomes neurologically real."[4] In fact, it has been shown that sustained daily prayer can produce physical changes in our brain noticeable enough to be seen and measured in comparative brain scans.[5] Prayer is capable of not only altering our brains; it can change our hearts, reducing stress and lowering blood pressure.

Even when prayer is an afterthought it seems it still has an afterglow, an afterlife all of its own. Praying in my tradition a certain liturgy at a certain moment in time, I know and find great solace in the notion that I join a whole host of other doubters and believers who pray at the same time the same words in time and space. And not only them but generations of doubters and believers from ages past as well as generations to come who pray and have prayed and will pray. My pitiful little petition somehow becomes interwoven in a richly embroidered eternal tapestry of all past, present, and future prayers. Any time I pray at the rising or setting of the sun I am joined by others who, in turn, face the same star and whisper a little hope or thanksgiving to the painted sky. And by witnessing and praying to the twilit skies of *this* day, my moments somehow become part of an ever unfolding primordial dusk and dawn, now and ever, and unto ages of ages.

Which isn't to say that prayer always comes from an awareness of that interconnection, or even from joyfulness; sometimes—often—prayer begins with doubt or pain. With eruption and upheaval and uncertainty. Ultimately, what colors our interior skies so beautifully—if prayer is our atmosphere—more often than not begins with some sort of disruption in our lives. We will not always have clear skies in life. There will be ashes. What matters is what we allow into our atmosphere; what we absorb, filter out, scatter, or reflect. The sun is always rising or setting somewhere, an eternal dawn and an eternal dusk. But it isn't the hereafter we should be after here. At the end of the day all we really have is right now, the time of our lives. By grace the now I intend to embody at my last breath will be different than the one I struggle to embody even now as I write these words.

And after?

---

4. Newberg and Waldman, *How God Changes Your Brain*, 3. See also Newberg et al., *Why God Won't Go Away*.

5. Ibid., 26–27.

Time, Twilight, and Eternity

I certainly cannot say with any certainty what comes after anything, especially life. All I know is in the beginning was mystery and in the end there is only mystery. If there is an afterlife I will only know for sure after death—my own. What's more important, I believe, lies in the in-between: not the promise of life everlasting so much as life at last. Every sunrise is a new beginning: we all arise with each dawn a rose resurrection.

And yet if here and now are all that really matter, I have no idea how to explain the before and after of my writing these words that are just now arriving at the neural pathways traversing your brain. What are we to make of this phenomenon: that you will read in your own present moment, after the fact, what I felt compelled to write in mine? That I felt so moved by a fleeting glimpse of something eternal in the twilit sky I thought to attempt to capture it in prose? Or my hope that someone, perhaps you, might also see in some other fiery sky a blazing reminder that this life, this breath, this now—whenever it is—is a stunningly remarkable and astonishing thing? Where does that place you and me in the before and after of human time, the you reading this now in your present moment in time, and the me who is writing this in yet another now, albeit one that is surely and already past?

Or what to do with the fact that I have been praying, not only over each of these words and pages that I might string them together correctly, but also for you long before you ever read them.

Bibliography

Abbott, Claude Colleer, ed. *The Correspondence of Gerard Manley Hopkins and Richard Watson Dixon*. London: University Press, 1935.
Abram, David. *The Spell of the Sensuous*. New York: Random House, 1996.
Aleichem, Sholem. *Tevye the Dairyman and the Railroad Stories*. Translated by Hillel Halkin. New York: Schocken, 1987.
Altick, Richard. "Four Victorian Poets and an Exploding Island." *Victorian Studies* 3 (March, 1960) 249–60.
Augustine of Hippo, *The Confessions of St. Augustine*. Translated by J. G. Pilkington. New York: Heritage, 1963.
Bachelard, Gaston. *The Flame of a Candle*. Translated by Joni Caldwell. Dallas: Dallas Institute Publications, 1988.
———. *The Poetics of Space*. Translated by Maria Jolas. Boston: Beacon, 1969.
Baer, Ulrich, ed. *The Poet's Guide to Life: The Wisdom of Rilke*. New York: Modern Library, 2012.
Barks, Coleman, and Michael Green. *The Illuminated Prayer: The Five-Times Prayer of the Sufis as Revealed by Jellaludin Rumi and Bawa Muhaiyaddeen*. New York: Ballantine Wellspring, 2000.
Barrie, J. M. *Peter Pan*. Buffalo: Broadview, 2011.
Bashō, Matsuo. *Narrow Road to the Interior and Other Writings*. Translated by Sam Hamill. Boston: Shambhala, 1991.
Basil of Caesarea. *St. Basil the Great, on the Holy Spirit*. Translated by D. Anderson. Crestwood: St. Vladimir's Seminary Press, 1980.
Blake, William. *The Complete Poetry and Prose of William Blake*. Berkeley: University of California Press, 2008.
Bly, Robert, ed. *The Winged Life: The Poetic Voice of Henry David Thoreau*. New York: HarperCollins, 1986.
The Book of Common Prayer and Administration of the Sacraments and Other Rites and Ceremonies of the Church. New York: Church Publishing, 1979.
Boorstin, Daniel. *The Discoverers: A History of Man's Search to Know His World and Himself*. New York: Random House, 1983.
Brother Lawrence. *Practice of the Presence of God*. Translated by Sr. Mary David. New York: Paulist, 1978.
Browning, Robert. *Robert Browning: Selected Poems*. London: Routledge, 2010.
Buber, Martin. *I and Thou*. Translated by Robert Gregor Smith. New York: Charles Scribner's Sons, 1958.

Carroll, Lewis. *Alice's Adventures in Wonderland* and *Through the Looking Glass and What Alice Found There*. New York: Barnes & Noble, 2012.
Chaliha, Jaya, and Edward LeJoly, eds. *Mother Teresa: The Joy in Loving, a Guide to Daily Living*. New York: Viking Penguin, 1996.
Cheever, Nancy, et al. "Out of Sight Is Not Out of Mind: The Impact of Restricting Wireless Mobile Device Use on Anxiety Levels Among Low, Moderate and High Users." In *Computers and Human Behavior*, 37 (2014) 290–97.
Chōmei, Kamo-no. *Hōjōki: Visions of a Torn World*. Translated by Yashuhiko Moriguchi and David Jenkins. Berkeley: Stone Bridge, 1996.
Cipolla, Carlo M. *Clocks and Culture: 1300–1700*. New York: Norton, 1978.
Comins, Neil F. *What If the Moon Didn't Exist?* New York: HarperCollins, 1993.
Darwin, Charles. *The Descent of Man*. Chicago: Brittanica, 1952.
———. *The Expression of Emotions in Man and Animals*. New York: Philosophical Library, 1955.
Dickinson, Emily. *The Collected Poems of Emily Dickinson*. New York: Barnes & Noble, 2003.
———. *Selected Poems*. New York: St. Martin's, 1992.
Dix, G. *The Apostolic Tradition of Hippolytus of Rome*. London: SPCK, 1937.
Dukas, Helen, and Banesh Hoffman. *Albert Einstein: The Human Side*. Princeton: Princeton University Press, 1979.
Eiseley, Loren. *The Firmament of Time*. New York: Atheneum, 1960.
Eliot, T. S. *Collected Poems 1909–1962*. New York: Harcourt Brace Jovanovich, 1963.
Emerson, Ralph Waldo. *The Complete Works of Ralph Waldo Emerson*. Boston: Houghton, Mifflin, 1904.
———. *The Journals of Ralph Waldo Emerson*. Boston: Houghton, Mifflin, 1914.
Flint, Kate. *The Victorians and the Visual Imagination*. Cambridge: Cambridge University Press, 2000.
Griffith, Ralph T. H. *Hymns of the Rig-Veda*. New Delhi: Munshiram Manoharlal, 1987.
Hanh, Thích Nhât. *Inside the Now: Meditations on Time*. Berkeley: Parallax, 2015.
———. *No Death, No Fear: Comforting Wisdom for Life*. New York: Riverhead, 2002.
———. *Present Moment, Wonderful Moment*. Berkeley: Parallax, 2002.
Heidegger, Martin. *On the Way to Language*. Translated by Peter D. Hertz. New York: Harper & Row, 1971.
Heschel, Abraham Joshua. *Man Is Not Alone: A Philosophy of Religion*. New York: Harper & Row, 1966.
———. *The Sabbath: Its Meaning for Modern Man*. New York: Farrar, Straus and Young, 1951.
———. *The Wisdom of Heschel*. Translated by Ruth M. Goodhill. New York: Macmillan, 1986.
Hoeppe, Götz. *Why the Sky Is Blue: Discovering the Color of Life*. Translated by John Stewart. Princeton: Princeton University Press, 2007.
Holmes, Oliver Wendell. *The Autocrat of the Breakfast-table*. Boston: Phillips, Sampson, 1858.
Hooper, Richard. *Jesus, Buddha, Krishna, Lao Tzu: The Parallel Sayings*. New York: Bristol Park, 2012.
Hopkins, Gerard Manley. *Gerard Manley Hopkins: The Major Works*. Oxford: Oxford University Press, 2009.

BIBLIOGRAPHY

Jewison, Norman, et al. *Fiddler on the Roof.* Beverly Hills: Twentieth Century Fox Home Entertainment, 2006.
Joyce, James. *Finnegan's Wake.* Oxford: Oxford University Press, 2012.
Kabir. *Kabir: Ecstatic Poems.* Translated by Robert Bly. Boston: Beacon, 2007.
Kairos Theologians. *The Kairos Document: Challenge to the Church: a Theological Comment on the Political Crisis in South Africa.* Grand Rapids: William B. Eerdmans, 1986.
Kardong, Terrence G. *Benedict's Rule: A Translation and Commentary.* Collegeville: The Liturgical Press, 1996.
Keller, David G. R. *Desert Banquet: A Year of Wisdom from the Desert Mothers and Fathers.* Collegeville: Liturgical Press, 2011.
Kelly, Thomas. *A Testament of Devotion.* New York: Harper & Brothers, 1941.
Khayyam, Omar. *The Ruba'iyat of Omar Khayyam.* Translated by Peter Avery and John Heath-Stubbs. Harmondsworth: Penguin, 1981.
Komachi, Ono-no, and Izumi Shikibu. *The Ink Dark Moon: Love Poems by Ono No Komachi and Izumi Shikibu, Women of the Ancient Court of Japan.* Translated by Jane Hirshfield and Mariko Aratani. New York: Vintage, 1990.
Kugler, Robert, and Patrick J. Hartin. *An Introduction to the Bible.* Grand Rapids: Eerdmans, 2009.
Lao Tzu, *Tao Te-Ching.* Translated by Stephen Mitchell. New York: Harper & Row, 1988.
Lundin, Roger. *Emily Dickinson and the Art of Belief.* Grand Rapids: Eerdmans, 1998.
Maclean, Norman. *A River Runs Through It and Other Stories.* Chicago: University of Chicago Press, 1976.
Martin, Walt, and Magda Ott. *The Philosophy of Albert Einstein: Writings on Art, Science, and Peace.* New York: Fall River, 2013.
McQuiston, John. *Always We Begin Again: The Benedictine Way of Living.* Harrisburg: Morehouse, 1996.
Meister Eckhart. *Sermons and Treatises.* Translated by Maurice O'C. Walshe. London: Watkins, 1981.
Merton, Thomas. *The Collected Poems of Thomas Merton.* New York: New Directions, 1977.
———. *A Search for Solitude, The Journals of Thomas Merton.* San Francisco: HarperSanFrancisco, 1996.
Negri, Paul, ed. *Metaphysical Poetry: An Anthology.* Mineola: Dover, 2002.
Nerburn, Kent. *The Soul of an Indian and Other Writings from Ohiyesa (Charles Alexander Eastman).* Novato: New World Library, 2001.
Newberg, Andrew, and Mark Robert Waldman. *How God Changes Your Brain: Breakthrough Findings from a Leading Neuroscientist.* New York: Ballantine, 2010.
Newberg, Andrew, et al. *Why God Won't Go Away: Brain Science & the Biology of Belief.* New York: Ballantine, 2001.
Nomura, Yushi. *Desert Wisdom.* Garden City: Doubleday, 1982.
Ovid, *The Metamorphoses.* Translated by Horace Gregory. New York: Viking, 1958.
Payne, Roger, *Among Whales.* New York: Scribners, 1995.
Poe, Edgar Allen. *Great Tales and Poems of Edgar Allen Poe.* New York: Pocket Books, 2007.
Polman, Bert, Marilyn Kay Stulken, and James Rawlings Sydnor, eds. *Amazing Grace: Hymn Texts for Devotional Use.* Louisville: Westminster John Knox, 1994.
Prayer Book for the New Year. Translated by A. Th. Philips. New York: Hebrew Publishing, 1931.

Rilke, Rainer Maria. *Letters to a Young Poet.* Translated by Mark Harman. Cambridge: Harvard University Press, 2011.

———. *Prayers of a Young Poet.* Translated by Mark S. Burrows. Brewster: Paraclete, 2013.

———. *Rilke's Book of Hours: Love Poems to God.* Translated by Anita Barrows and Joanna Macy. New York: Riverhead, 2005.

Roberts, A., and J. Donaldson. *The Ante-Nicene Fathers, Vol III: Latin Christianity: It's Founder, Tertullian.* New York: Charles Scribner's Sons, 1926.

Rock, Thom. *Blueberry Fool: Memory, Moments, and Meaning.* Eugene: Wipf and Stock, 2011.

Rosen, L. D., et al. *iDisorder: Understanding Our Obsession with Technology and Overcoming Its Hold on Us.* New York: Palgrave-MacMillan, 2012.

Rumi, Jalal al-Din. *The Essential Rumi.* Translated by Coleman Barks. New York: HarperCollins, 2010.

———. *The Soul of Rumi: A New Collection of Ecstatic Poems.* Translated by Coleman Barks. New York: HarperCollins, 2001.

Seow, C. L. *Job 1–21: Interpretation and Commentary.* Grand Rapids: Eerdmans, 2013.

Shakespeare, William. *The Complete Works.* New York: Harcourt, Brace & World, 1952.

Shapley, Harlow. *Beyond the Observatory.* New York: Charles Scribner's Sons, 1967.

Stager, Curt. *Your Atomic Self: The Invisible Elements That Connect You to Everything Else in the Universe.* New York: St. Martin's, 2014.

Star, Jonathan. *Two Stars Rising: A Collection of Sacred Writings.* New York: Bantam, 1991.

Stern, Anthony. *Everything Starts from Prayer: Mother Teresa's Meditations on Spiritual Life for People of All Faiths.* New York: MJF Books, 2009.

Stern, Chaim, ed. *Gates of Prayer: The New Union Prayerbook.* New York: Central Conference of American Rabbis, 1975.

Strand, Clark. *Waking Up to the Dark: Ancient Wisdom for a Sleepless Age.* New York: Spiegel & Grau, 2015.

Teilhard de Chardin, Pierre. *Toward the Future.* New York: Harcourt, 1973.

Teresa of Ávila. *The Interior Castle.* Translated by The Benedictines of Stanbrook. New York: Barnes & Noble, 2005.

Thompson, Richard. *Monet to Matisse: Landscape Painting in France 1874–1914.* Edinburgh: National Gallery of Scotland, 1994.

Thoreau, Henry David. *The Journal: 1837–1861.* New York: New York Review, 2009.

———. *Walking.* Rockville: Arc Manor, 2007.

Tolle, Eckhart. *The Power of Now: A Guide to Spiritual Enlightenment.* Novato: New World Library, 2004.

Uspensky, Nicholas. *Evening Worship in the Orthodox Church.* Translated by Paul Lazor. Crestwood: St. Vladimir's Seminary Press, 1985.

Vaughan-Lee, Llewellyn. *Love Is a Fire: The Sufi's Mystical Journey Home.* Inverness: The Golden Sufi Center, 2000.

Van Gogh, Vincent. *The Complete Letters of Vincent van Gogh.* Greenwich: New York Graphic Society, 1958.

Walker, Alice. *The Color Purple.* New York: Harcourt, 1982.

Weil, Simone. *Waiting for God.* New York: HarperCollins, 2001.

Welty, Eudora. *One Writer's Beginnings.* Cambridge: Harvard University Press, 2000.

Werness, Hope. "Whitman and van Gogh: Starry Nights and Other Similarities." *Walt Whitman Quarterly Review* 2, no. 4 (Spring, 1985) 35–41.

Wesley, John. *The Works of John Wesley.* Nashville: Abingdon, 1984.

Bibliography

Whitman, Walt. *Leaves of Grass*. New York: Barnes & Noble, 1993.
Wilkinson, J. *Egeria's Travels*. London: S.P.C.K., 1971.
Zicheng, Hong. *Caigentan*. Translated by Robert Aiken and Daniel W. Kwok. Washington, D.C.: Shoemaker Hoard, 2006.

www.ingramcontent.com/pod-product-compliance
Lightning Source LLC
Chambersburg PA
CBHW050823160426
43192CB00010B/1876